I0368487

THE UNIVERSITY OF QUEENSLAND
AUSTRALIA

CREATE CHANGE

Wellbeing Polarity Leadership: How Young Leaders Can Impact the 21st Century

Dr Lance R. Newey, Dawn Boland, Lara Berge

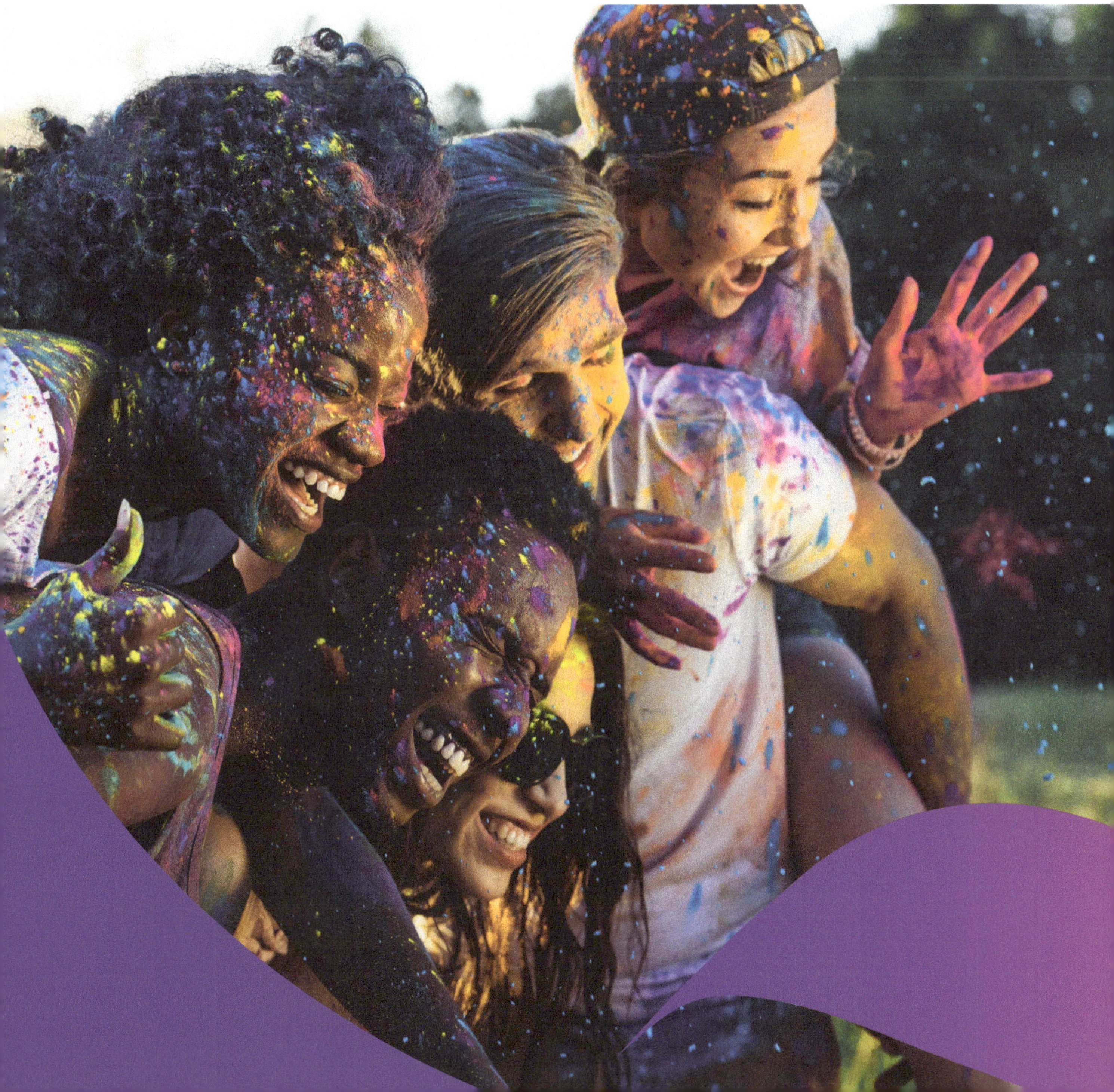

 A catalogue record for this book is available from the National Library of Australia

Copyright © 2024 by Dr Lance R. Newey, Dawn Boland, Lara Berge

All rights reserved. No part of this book may be reproduced or transmitted in any form or by any means, electronic or mechanical, including photocopying, recording, or by any information storage and retrieval system, without permission in writing from the copyright owner.

Publisher:
Inspiring Publishers
P.O. Box 159, Calwell, ACT Australia 2905
Email: inspiringpublisher.com
http://www.inspiringpublishers.com

National Library of Australia Cataloguing-in-Publication entry

Author: Dr Lance R. Newey, Dawn Boland, Lara Berge

Title: Wellbeing Polarity Leadership: How Young Leaders Can Impact the 21st Century

ISBN: 978-1-923087-78-1 (print)
ISBN: 978-1-923087-77-4 (ePub2)
ISBN: 978-1-923087-76-7 (PDF eBook)

Dedication

I dedicate this book to the many students over the years, including Dawn and Lara, who I have had the pleasure of sharing the classroom with. We have shared the mission of not just accepting the world as it is but rather to be a force for nudging it in better directions with better answers. Thank you for making Education such a rewarding profession.

The book is also dedicated to my wife who encourages me through thick and thin and is my best sales rep! Also my little boy who I love more than there are stars in the sky. May this book be a little light along the way of your path.

LN

Our pathway in this book

03
FOREWORD

04
INTRODUCTION
Why we need wellbeing polarity leadership

Central message
Our opportunity
A book for parents and their young leaders
Connections to wellbeing
New learnings

13
THEORY
Learning the fundamentals

Our research
Vertical spiral of development
Wellbeing polarity leadership—key concepts
Wholeness—tuning into our parts
Practical exercise—wholeness clock: Where have I been spending my time today?
The big switch that wellbeing leaders make
Counter-balance and polarities
How one-sidedness affects everything
The link between wholeness and polarities

27
PRACTICAL
Building wellbeing polarity leadership competency

Wellbeing polarity leadership competency 1: How's my within-component counterbalance?
Balancing within components
Valuing our polarities
Wellbeing polarity leadership competency 2: How's my across-component counterbalance?
Balancing across components
Wellbeing polarity leadership competency 3: Wellbeing leadership in action
Back to technical and adaptive challenges

37
PERSONAL DEVELOPMENT
Help for making your personal leadership changes

The process of inner change
Hero and the dragon
Practical exercise: reflection on experience
Frequently asked questions
Wall poster

45
APPENDIX
Practical exercises for building competencies in the components of wellbeing

Foreword

The complexity and distractions of the modern world are daily realities for our students. These influences come from all directions and represent both overt and covert attacks on the mental health and well-being of the students.

At a time in life when students are endeavouring to establish their adult identities and determine their tribe, this undermining and ambiguity add complexity to an already challenging stage of life. Schools are often the most stable and safe space in students' lives. They use this safe space to seek clarity and affirmation of their developing identity from their peers and trusted teachers.

Schools play a crucial role in fostering a confident, positive identity for our students. This is achieved through both the structured and hidden curriculum, interwoven with many co-curricular and extra-curricular activities, as well as sporting and artistic pursuits. This book, along with the domains of the Well-being Polarity Leadership model, provides schools with a future-focused model. As previously mentioned, our students are constantly exposed to negative influences that diminish them. Consequently, supporting student well-being is a priority for every school. Integrating such an approach into an already packed curriculum is always challenging. We recognise that any 'bolt-on' program will fail. This model, with its eight components of well-being or polarities, offers a framework and language accessible to students across various age groups. It equips schools and teachers with the terminology to build understanding with their students and serves as a practical model to explore scenarios and conflicts that might emerge in class or from life challenges students face. Viewing adversities as polarities—aspects of life that are simply out of balance but rectifiable—enables a more solution-focused approach in analysis and discussion.

The benefit for schools, and our future leaders, is that they have a 21st-century, contextually relevant well-being model that offers a reference point for students to assess their current challenges. By reconceptualising problems as mere polarity imbalances in our life well-being components, and understanding that these polarities can sometimes be rebalanced with minor interventions, anxiety can be reduced. By addressing the polarity imbalance, students can identify effective, and hopefully easily enacted, solutions.

I urge schools to adopt this fresh approach to the well-being and leadership development opportunities you provide for our students. It's a critically important endeavour for the student body in every school, especially in these times when apt and targeted resources are limited. Equipping our students with models and language to navigate their increasingly intricate world will boost their well-being, ensuring they are best positioned to maximise their potential. The challenge for schools lies in integrating this approach, along with its associated thought processes and language, into their institutional narrative and culture for the betterment of their student body.

Liew Paulger | College Executive Principal (2015–2022)
Kelvin Grove State College

This book is the result of a research collaboration between the University of Queensland Business School and:

Kelvin Grove State College   **John Paul College**   **Indooroopilly State High**   **Ironside Primary**

As such, the work is a pioneering initiative across all levels of the education system in an effort to develop a new generation of wellbeing polarity leaders. We have taken university-level research and made its benefits available to parents and young emerging leaders. Because we believe that educators, parents, and young emerging leaders can be wellbeing polarity leaders for the 21st century!

Introduction

Why we need **wellbeing polarity leadership**

In his 90th year, I asked my Dad what he thought was most important in life. There's a usual bunch of answers to this question—having children, raising a family, achievement, wealth, career—but he mentioned none of those things. He said, 'Health, because you're no good to anybody without it'. There's a lot of great wisdom in that answer. Thanks, Dad.

This book is about wellbeing, which encompasses health but also extends beyond it. The figure below, which we've dubbed the 'Wellbeing Polarity Wheel1', illustrates eight components of wellbeing: economic, environmental, social, cultural, material, physical, psychological, and spiritual. We'll delve into these in greater detail as we progress. In this book, wellbeing signifies the capacity to thrive resiliently within and across these components. Two pivotal terms to note here: thrive and resiliently.

Thriving denotes enjoying a full life, while resilience acknowledges that at times our wellbeing might suffer setbacks, necessitating our ability to bounce back. What's your interpretation of wellbeing? Notably, our research posed this question to numerous leaders from business, government, and not-for-profit sectors. Their responses are vital, as our perception of wellbeing can influence the extent to which we experience it, or lack thereof.

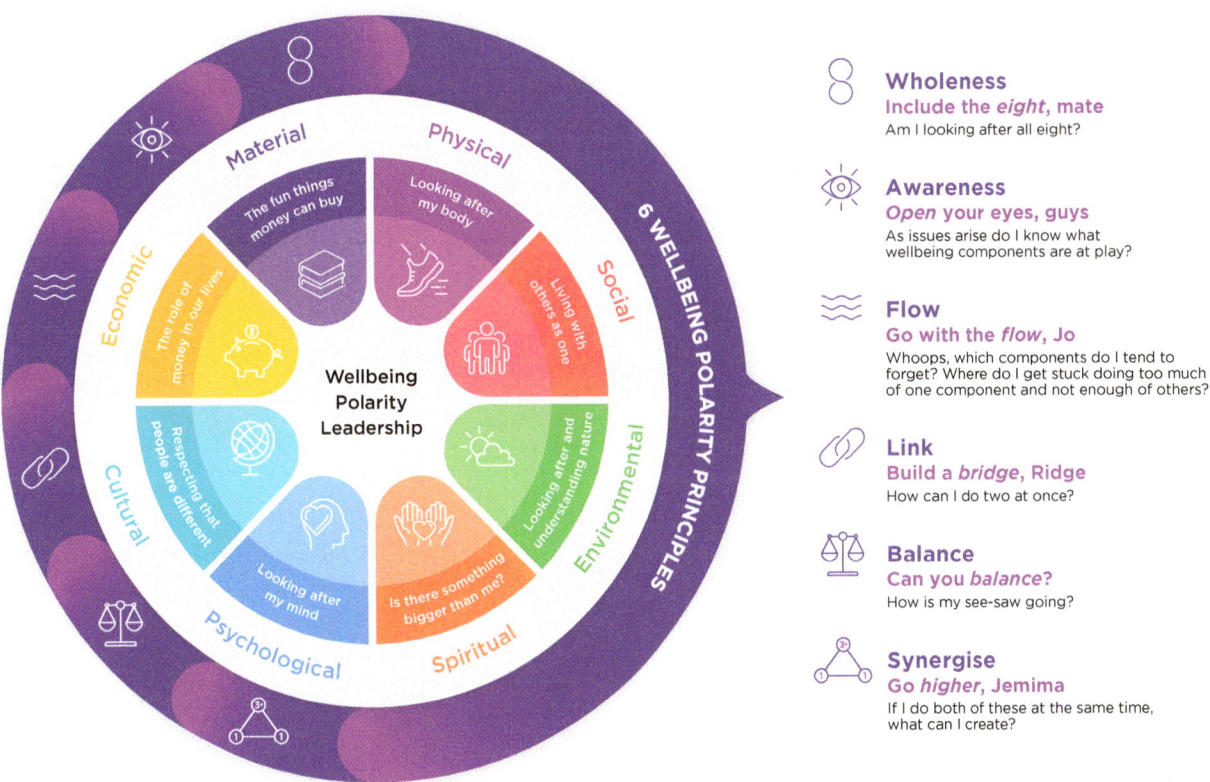

1   To ensure your wellbeing is consistent/best to deal with the daily challenges/changes of life we recommend using the 'Wellbeing Polarity Wheel' as a poster on the walls of office spaces, classrooms and/or bedrooms.

Central message

The central message of our book is that, based on the findings of our research with leaders across the world, 21st-century wellbeing for individuals, families, businesses, and societies can benefit from a different type of leader—a wellbeing polarity leader.

Wellbeing polarity leaders make wellbeing their central mission in everything they do. However, our research shows that to make this a reality, we must do some things differently—look after all eight components and counter-balance them. Counter-balance means that the components can work as opposites to each other. This defines a polarity—two opposing values that need each other to co-exist, despite seeming contradictory.

A contemporary example is how businesses need to earn money by producing and selling goods and services (economic wellbeing) while simultaneously doing so in a manner that looks after the environment sustainably (environmental wellbeing). During a pandemic, there's a need to keep people protected, safe, and healthy (physical wellbeing) while also striving to keep economies open (economic wellbeing). Wellbeing, therefore, becomes a delicate balancing act.

Wellbeing challenges us to become comfortable with polarities (contradictions)—maintaining a balance between two opposing aspects simultaneously. This doesn't come naturally to many, as we often seek solutions with just one correct answer—like locking down a city to ensure physical wellbeing. However, many leaders have realised that managing polarities requires us to think differently. Hence, there's a need for guidance. This book provides that guidance. Its aim is to encourage parents and young emerging leaders to engage in wellbeing conversations, using the presented ideas as discussion points.

The issue

Life consistently presents challenges to our wellbeing. Intriguingly, these very challenges can serve as profound teachers about wellbeing—defining what it is, how to foster it, and what undermines it. Our research into these issues reveals a need for leaders who can discern what these challenges are teaching us about wellbeing. We've found that we often lean towards one-sidedness. One-sidedness is when we excessively prioritise certain facets of wellbeing over others. This overlooks the essential nature of wellbeing, which involves managing polarities and counter-balancing various aspects. This imbalance manifests in our personal lives, the way businesses function, and the numerous societal issues plaguing our communities.

Failing to acknowledge wellbeing polarities can lead to escalating problems. However, as we'll explore, the reverse is also true: a minor change in wellbeing practice by a group of 100 like-minded individuals can precipitate a significant global shift. **Change is possible!**

Mmmm, please stop and think for a moment.

Where in my life are things not going so well? Is this an adaptive challenge with a contradiction I'm not playing so well?

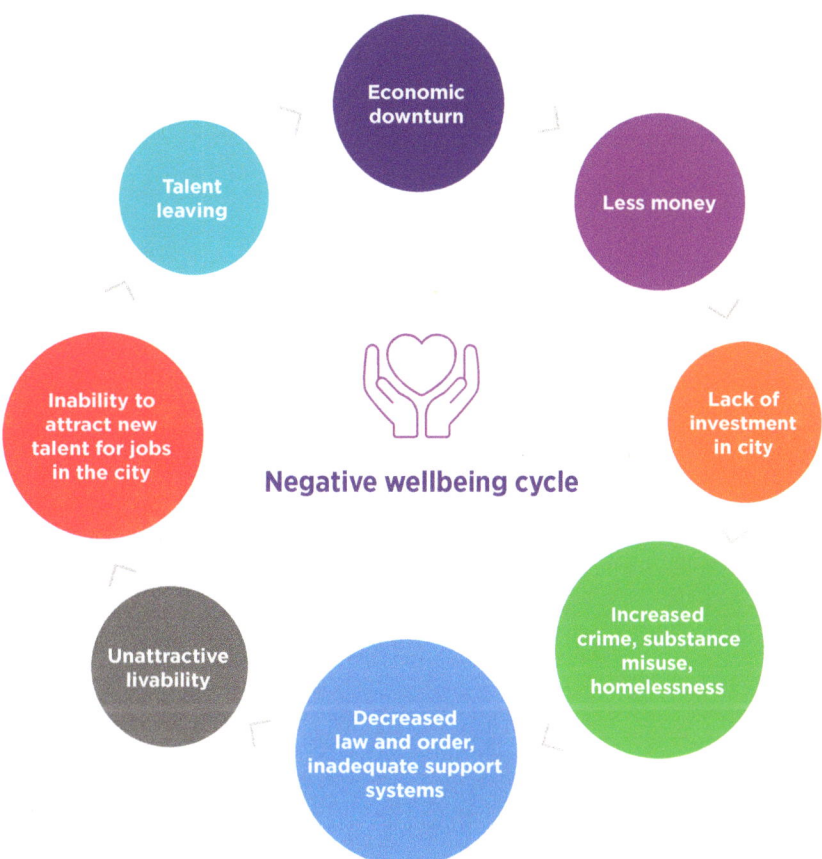

Why one-sidedness is a big problem—negative wellbeing cycles

Let's take a deeper look at negative compounding effects. We aim to illustrate how one wellbeing issue can trigger others in a downward spiral. Have you ever considered how cities either enhance or harm the wellbeing of their residents? One city we collaborate with has exhibited one-sidedness, basing its economic health solely on the oil industry. This approach made the city immensely prosperous. However, when the oil industry declined, the city faced a cascade of subsequent challenges, jeopardising its survival. We've identified this pattern as a negative wellbeing cycle.

When a city loses its primary industry, taxation revenue plummets. This downturn, coupled with a lack of community-mindedness, has resulted in the city's deterioration. Reduced government funds mean limited expenditure on policing and the justice system, paving the way for crime and substance misuse to flourish. Such circumstances make a locale unappealing for habitation, thus deterring business investment and the influx of new talent – the young individuals essential for accomplishing basic tasks and delivering services. Compounding residents' dismay, their Young Emerging Leaders are also departing, disillusioned by the city's diminished livability. This predicament stems from the city's initial one-sidedness – metaphorically speaking, placing all their eggs in the oil basket. The key takeaway is that all eight wellbeing components are interrelated; a decline in one can instigate a slump in the others. To redirect the narrative for cities like this, we need wellbeing polarity leaders.

A KEY DISTINCTION

So, where does one-sidedness originate? We've pinpointed two primary culprits:

- We're trained as specialists in our selected fields, potentially narrowing our perspective to that specialisation exclusively.
- Contradictions create discomfort, and we're naturally inclined to sidestep such unease.

As we'll discuss, contradictions are vital to wellbeing. To comprehend this, let's explore what Harvard Professor Ronald Heifetz[2] delineates as the distinction between technical problems and adaptive challenges. Technical problems possess identifiable causes and solutions; one simply applies expertise to resolve the issue. Developing a COVID-19 vaccine serves as a pertinent example.

Conversely, adaptive challenges are inherently complex. Their origins may remain elusive, and straightforward solutions are absent. These challenges might encompass contradictions, like determining whether to maintain business operations during a pandemic or instate closures to safeguard public health. Occasionally, when confronted with such adaptive challenges, we might gravitate towards one extreme, resulting in polarisation – two opposing factions at odds. Yet, adaptive challenges demand an alternative mindset. To adeptly manoeuvre through these challenges, our Young Emerging Leaders must grow comfortable with contradictions!

---

2 Heifetz, R. 1997. The Work of Leadership. *Harvard Business Review* (January-February); 1994. Leadership Without Easy Answers : Cambridge, MA: Harvard Business School Press

Our **opportunity**

The opportunity we have, then, is to place our ground-breaking research into the hands of parents and Young Emerging Leaders, allowing us all to tune in to a fresh perspective on the vital lessons our current world is teaching us about the adaptive challenges of wellbeing.

We have the opportunity to correct our one-sidedness and instead become wellbeing polarity leaders. Specifically, our research indicates that we need a new generation of leader who can:

- Overcome one-sidedness;
- Be aware of and value the eight components of wellbeing;
- Commit to counter-balancing opposing components (polarities) of wellbeing instead of choosing sides.

Allow yourself the opportunity to explore what this means for you! This suggests that anyone can be a wellbeing polarity leader. While some wellbeing polarity leaders may have a formal role as a leader and can use this learning to benefit themselves and others, even if you're not in a formal leadership position, wellbeing polarity leadership concerns how you lead yourself. This includes what you prioritise in your life, how you resolve conflicts, form opinions, and navigate life's learning curves. Adopting wellbeing polarity leadership as part of your mindset means you'll make a different impact on the world. Your own wellbeing will influence others and their wellbeing. Using the content in this book, you'll evolve into a better employee, friend, partner, son/daughter, parent, and leader.

Self-efficacy—yes, you can do it!

You're not alone. Numerous individuals, just like you, aim to enact positive change in their lives, the lives of others, and the broader world. Age, experience, financial standing, or cultural background doesn't matter; your passion and drive make all the difference in terms of wellbeing. While such responsibility can seem daunting, remember that even a minor change, when combined with countless others, results in a significant positive shift in our world. For students, parents, and teachers, almost every government, organisation, company, or institution, from grassroots to global levels, acknowledges that wellbeing is crucial for human flourishing and solution creation for a better world.

In today's context, amidst numerous statements, policies, and frameworks, it can be challenging to find a path that fosters self-efficacy (the belief that you can achieve something) and offers methods to cultivate wellbeing. This book serves as a tool to boost our self-efficacy and guide us in creating positive change opportunities during trying times.

Our point of difference

While many equate wellbeing solely with wellness—both mental and physical—our research presents a broader perspective. Such a narrow view doesn't foster the kind of wellbeing polarity leaders we need for 21st-century adaptive challenges. Our model:

- Encompasses eight components of wellbeing that require dynamic balance: economic, environmental, social, cultural, physical, psychological, spiritual, and material. Paying attention to these prepares us to be effective wellbeing polarity leaders;
- Stresses the significance of polarities by counter-balancing the eight components. Optimal wellbeing is achieved through this counter-balancing ability. Many modern challenges—excessive oceanic plastic, stress, burnout, mental health issues, racism, and a dearth of community-mindedness—all suggest an overemphasis on one type of wellbeing at the expense of another.

Traditional models, employed by various organisations and institutions, often approach wellbeing in a compartmentalised and linear fashion, aiming at single wellbeing facets. Contrarily, the wellbeing wheel endorses a holistic, balanced approach, adapted to today's unique global challenges. It isn't an all-or-nothing approach. Wellbeing isn't a simple puzzle to be solved and discarded; it's an ever-evolving, intricate concept demanding regular monitoring, subtle adjustments, and everyone's dedication to instigate positive change.

A book for parents/caregivers

Why a book for both parents/caregivers and their young leaders as the audience? Because wellbeing can be a central value in our families. Indeed, our hope is to encourage 'wellbeing conversations' in families.

This book can be used to develop a wellbeing language within the family and to enhance our awareness of wellbeing in our daily lives. Our aim isn't to preach what is right, but to guide wellbeing conversations in directions that are deeper and more meaningful than our current discussions.

Message for parents/caregivers

We all aspire for our Young Emerging Leaders to thrive. Amidst life's chaos, we often wish for a straightforward guide to reassure us that our Young Emerging Leaders are navigating our intricate world effectively. This guide, informed by our experiences as educators, acknowledges the wellbeing challenges many Young Emerging Leaders face upon entering university. We believe we aren't equipping them sufficiently to manage their personal challenges, let alone those posed by the broader world. However, the silver lining is our research can guide us in cultivating better wellbeing for individuals, businesses, and societies. What could be a more valuable investment than bolstering the wellbeing of our Young Emerging Leaders?

Message for young emerging leaders

Life is a canvas for great dreams to materialise. Along the journey, myriad challenges confront us. At times, making sense of it all can seem daunting. One certainty emerges: to realise your dreams, wellbeing is paramount. How can we nurture our wellbeing and that of others in today's ever-evolving world? We invite you to embrace our novel approach to wellbeing. Harness its uncomplicated yet potent principles to navigate the myriad wellbeing challenges our world throws your way. Become a wellbeing polarity leader!

Our vision

That our parents/caregivers feel confident they are building wellbeing polarity leaders for our world.

That young emerging leaders learn to read the pattern of wellbeing issues around them and be able to shift towards better wellbeing.

Wellbeing conversation opportunities

One of our key aims with this book is to encourage deeper wellbeing conversations between parents, caregivers and young emerging leaders. To help with this we have included prompts in various places to show how the content in that section represents a 'wellbeing conversation opportunity'.

Look out for the conversation symbol for conversation prompts.

Connections to **wellbeing**

In the school curriculum, organisations and governments

'Wellbeing' is a 'buzzword' frequently encountered in literature from a variety of sources. However, wellbeing isn't a magic wand that we can simply wave. Merely having a policy or framework highlighting the importance of wellbeing doesn't guarantee its automatic manifestation.

Wellbeing has different aspects, these are delicately balanced symbiotic relationships that interact and interrelate. Wellbeing is something we need to speak about and have a common understanding of. Wellbeing is something that needs to be monitored and checked, that we are all responsible for, to ourselves and each other, to ensure that we can bring about positive change to the whole world.

The diagram below illustrates some of the connections to wellbeing that influence the thinking of our students, parents, and teachers. Each group has unique perspectives or expectations regarding wellbeing, warranting its incorporation into a framework or policy.

Navigating such an overcrowded system can be difficult to navigate. How can I make sense of it?

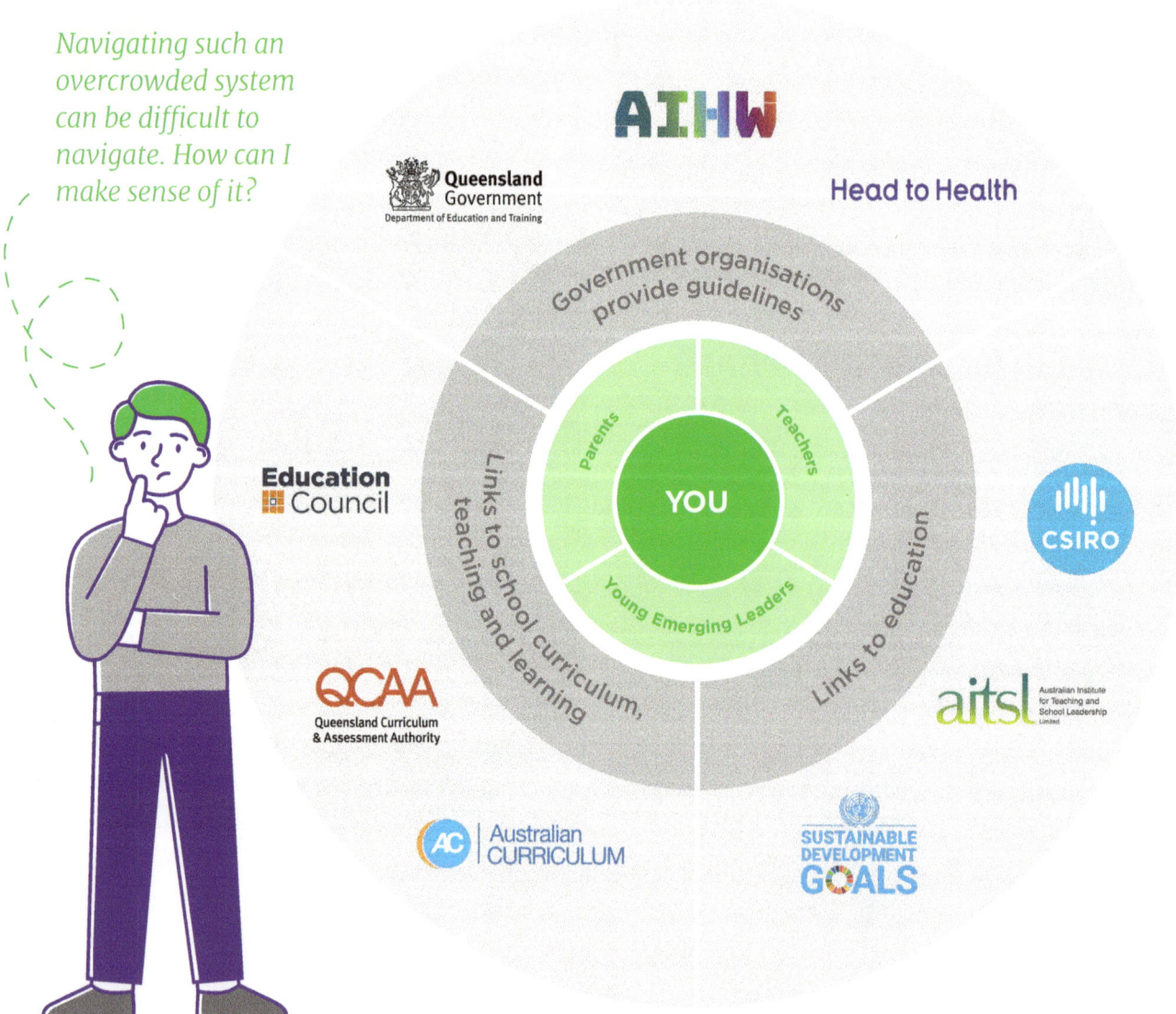

12   Wellbeing Polarity Leadership: How Young Leaders Can Impact the 21st Century

New **learnings**

OK, our upcoming sections delve into new learnings. Think of it as an adventure. Each section comes with a learning objective, serving as a guide to help us concentrate on the key points presented.

The challenge lies in the fact that the material will stretch your thinking, taking you into unfamiliar territory. However, rest assured, we aren't venturing into this new realm alone; we have two guides to assist us...

Sally has extensive experience venturing into wild places. She relishes the challenge of navigating the jungle, which gives her a profound sense of accomplishment. Charge on, Sally!

Daniel recognises that leadership requires a bit of additional effort. He's prepared to go those extra metres to develop further and realise his potential. Go, Daniel!

Who **am I?**

Before we begin, we'd like to introduce a valuable exercise titled 'Who am I?'. Both parents and young emerging leaders can complete this.

The questions below provide an opportunity for self-reflection on our current beliefs before we delve into this book. Please jot down your answers. **After** working through the book, you'll find a section titled 'Revised Who am I?'. Answer the questions in that section and then compare your responses with the ones you noted at the outset. This exercise effectively highlights the impact of this book on us, revealing whether it has influenced or even altered our identities and how we present ourselves to the world.

1. In your own words, how would you define wellbeing?
2. In your own words, how would you define leadership?
3. What do you think makes a great leader?
4. Do you consider yourself a leader? If not, why not?
5. Which of your own character strengths are you most grateful for?
6. What do you value most in life?

A helpful exercise here if you're not too sure is to google 'list of values' and print a near exhaustive list of ~300 values. Then, go through them crossing things out that don't resonate, until you're left with three or four that really do.

7. What are the experiences that have impacted you the most in your life?
8. When do you feel most uncomfortable and why?
9. What would you like to change about yourself?
10. How do you view challenges in life? Are they avoidable? Are they helpful?
11. What is a challenge that you're currently facing?
12. What is a challenge that your city, community or school is currently facing? (e.g. how might we maintain economic prosperity while keeping the community safe?)
13. What types of conversation do you find most difficult to have? What's a conversation that you've found difficult to have with someone in your life?

Theory

Learning the **fundamentals**

Our **research**

 **Learning objective**

Understand the three types of wellbeing leader

Did you know that Leaders think very differently about what wellbeing is? We conducted an international study of 120 leaders[3] from India, Alaska and Norway. We chose India, Alaska and Norway because these three locations are usually at low, medium and high levels respectively on international wellbeing scales.

We aimed to gain insights into the perspectives on wellbeing across different countries. We surveyed all 120 leaders and subsequently conducted in-depth interviews with 65 of these leaders3. These leaders hailed from the business realm, governments, and the not-for-profit sector.

Intriguingly, our research identified three types of wellbeing leaders: Simplifiers, Accommodators, and Embracers. We discerned these types by presenting leaders with the eight-component wellbeing wheel, which we introduced at the beginning of the book, and inquiring about which components they integrate into their work.

What underlies these varied approaches to wellbeing? The determining factor appears to be a leader's capability to handle complexity. Not all leaders are at ease contemplating all eight components. Some find it overwhelming, while others navigate it with ease. What emerges distinctly is that 21st-century adaptive challenges necessitate a greater presence of the third type of leader: the Embracers.

Wow, I didn't realise people think so differently about wellbeing.

WELLBEING CONVERSATION OPPORTUNITY

Which type of wellbeing leader do I and my parents/caregivers subscribe to?

---

[3] Mishra, A. (2022). 'How and Why Senior Managers Think Differently About Wellbeing: Towards a Constructive-Developmental Theory'. Unpublished PhD Dissertation, UQ Business School, University of Queensland.

Simplifiers

The first type of wellbeing leader deals with complexity by simplifying it.

They achieve this by not viewing wellbeing as their responsibility, something they don't need to consider. 'My job is just to make money' typifies this approach. These leaders tend to prioritise economic wellbeing above all other components. 'If the money is right, then everything else will follow' encapsulates their mindset. Wellbeing is primarily perceived as one's health — both mental and physical. Consequently, it's regarded as a personal responsibility and something individuals address at home.

These leaders see wellbeing and work like this:

Work and wellbeing are totally separate. Wellbeing is something you do at home.

Accommodators

The second type of wellbeing leader deals with complexity by accommodating some of the components in the workplace.

These leaders recognise that caring for people's mental and physical health, demonstrating social responsibility, and nurturing the natural environment also make sound business sense. These leaders accommodate more components than the first type and assume some responsibility for wellbeing at work.

These leaders see work and wellbeing like this:

Some components of wellbeing included at work: eg. economic, social, environmental, physical.

Embracers

The third type of wellbeing leader is a wellbeing polarity leader.

These leaders manage complexity by embracing all eight components in the workplace. They've come to recognise that all components are interdependent. Neglecting any one of them ultimately incurs a cost.

This third group of Leaders see work and wellbeing as one and the same:

Wellbeing and work are the same thing. All eight components included at work.

Vertical spiral of **development**

🎯 Learning objective

Understand the vertical spiral of development

Another insight we've gained is that leaders undergo a process of transformation to progress from the first type to the second and then to the third.

That is, they have encountered a disruptive event which caused them to reconsider one perspective on wellbeing and adopt another. The pattern appears to be a vertical spiral of development, as illustrated in the figure below. Observe how the spiral broadens as it ascends. This symbolises that, at each level of the spiral, leaders can consider an increasing number of wellbeing components. This spiral seems to represent an ongoing evolution. Issues arise when leaders adhere to a wellbeing perspective that doesn't align with the demands of their challenges.

Why would beliefs about wellbeing evolve in stages? The answer seems to lie in the idea that stages facilitate the incremental development of the capacity to comprehend increasingly complex views on wellbeing. Individuals can only manage a certain level of complexity at any given point, much like how our education system is divided into stages, e.g., Year 10, Year 11, Year 12, etc. However, as they become accustomed to one stage, a catalyst emerges, prompting new growth and fresh perspectives. This pattern also showcases an expanding recognition of the interconnectedness of all things. These notions are supported by research in the field of developmental psychology.

Daniel reckons 'no pain, no gain'

The vertical spiral of development

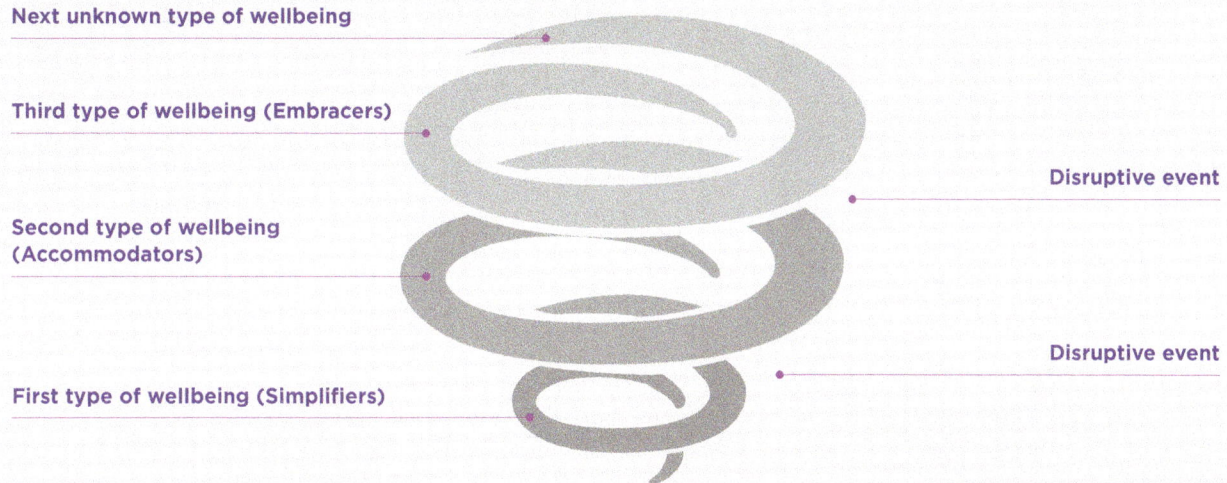

- Next unknown type of wellbeing
- Third type of wellbeing (Embracers)
- Second type of wellbeing (Accommodators)
- First type of wellbeing (Simplifiers)
- Disruptive event
- Disruptive event

What does this mean for wellbeing polarity leadership?

It's essential to recognise that individuals have varying capacities to process complexity. We can't expect everyone to manage all eight components. We need to engage with people based on their current complexity-processing abilities. Leaders, therefore, must oversee the entire spiral of varying beliefs, guiding individuals towards their next level of understanding. This means not attempting to coerce everyone into adopting the most intricate views of wellbeing. Wellbeing polarity leadership is about facilitating individual development in phases. As wellbeing polarity leaders, understanding these stages proves invaluable, offering a roadmap to support people on their journey to comprehend wellbeing. We learn to value stages of development and provide assistance as individuals transition from one stage to the next.

WELLBEING CONVERSATION OPPORTUNITY

The hidden gold in disruptive events and developmental difficulties

Many of us desire a trouble-free life. In fact, we often strive to evade challenges, aiming to constantly maintain a positive well-being and project a favourable social impression. A widely held belief is that life's adversities should be sidestepped and the ideal life is perpetually marked by success.

However, research in adult developmental psychology suggests that genuine, profound self-transformation often stems from life's trials and conflicts. From this perspective, while certain adversities should undoubtedly be avoided, some difficulties are inherently developmental. These challenges emerge to challenge our perceptions of ourselves, others, and the world at large. They urge us to re-evaluate our way of life. Instead of viewing them as negative, we should embrace these situations, pondering: "What is this experience teaching me about wellbeing?"

It's beneficial to allow developmental challenges to linger, despite the discomfort they may bring. Embrace them, delve into their significance, and allow them to reshape you. Such an approach distinguishes the Embracers.

Ask yourself: What current challenges am I or my family facing that could serve as developmental opportunities to deepen our understanding of wellbeing?

Wellbeing polarity leadership—**key concepts**

 **Learning objective**

Understand the key concepts that make up the 'language' of wellbeing polarity leadership

Wellbeing Polarity Leadership is the process of consciously making wellbeing our central mission, be it as individuals, families, businesses, or societies.

Wellbeing Components are distinct aspects of wellbeing that reside in all of us and influence our highs and lows.

Wholeness is the wellbeing principle that emphasises the need to address the eight components as a holistic entity.

Counterbalance is the wellbeing principle that necessitates maintaining opposing wellbeing components in a dynamic equilibrium.

Wellbeing Polarities are pairs of opposite yet positive values within or across wellbeing components that rely on each other for coexistence. For instance, when businesses need to produce goods and services while also preserving the natural environment. Wellbeing polarities are NOT contrasting values of positive and negative (good and bad). They are complementary, signifying the importance of both.

Competencies refer to specific skills and abilities needed within and across the components of wellbeing. (Refer to the Appendix for practical competency-building exercises).

Awareness is the continual capacity to identify our opportunities for wellbeing and to discern indicators of wellbeing issues.

Flow signifies the ability to seamlessly transition between two sides of a wellbeing polarity, e.g., between social and environmental wellbeing.

Early Warning Signs are indicators that signal when we are disproportionately prioritising certain components over others. For instance, a symptom of overvaluing economic wellbeing at a corporate level might be staff experiencing burnout or feeling demotivated.

Vertical Development is a continuous process of broadening one's perspective on wellbeing to increasingly consider multiple components when acting as a leader.

Disruptive Events or Developmental Difficulties are catalysts prompting a fundamental shift in one's view of wellbeing. Such events might include a health crisis, a yearning for greater life purpose, or a disagreement with a friend or family member

WELLBEING CONVERSATION OPPORTUNITY

How can my parents/caregivers and I include this wellbeing language in our lives and experiences?

I love to learn a new language!

Wholeness—
tuning in to our parts

 **Learning objective**

For wholeness, understand each of the eight components and how they speak to us

It is helpful to think of all the eight components as parts of us that send us messages. Wholeness then is paying attention to all eight and learning to read their messages.

When things aren't going so well they try to teach us something through the problems and adaptive challenges that come our way. Problems and adaptive challenges are teachers. Here is an example of the way our parts communicate with us and ask for a better relationship:

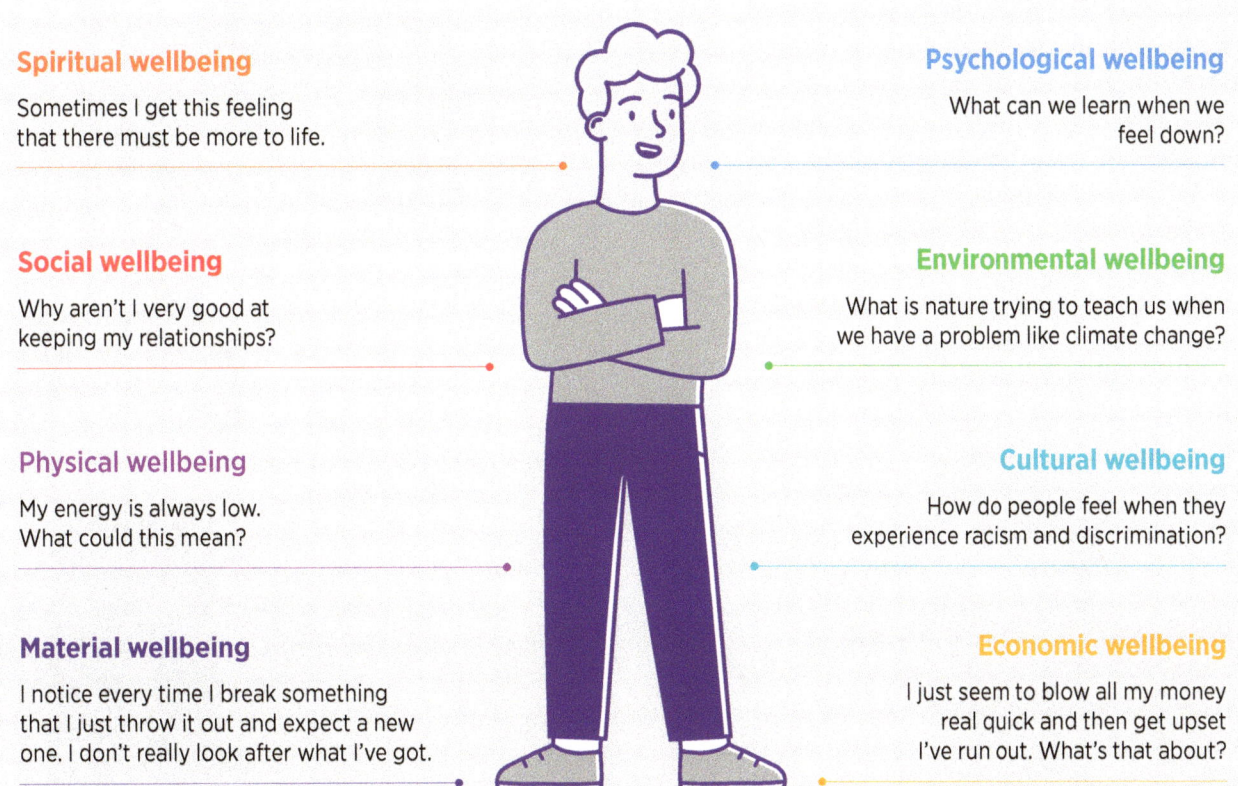

Spiritual wellbeing
Sometimes I get this feeling that there must be more to life.

Social wellbeing
Why aren't I very good at keeping my relationships?

Physical wellbeing
My energy is always low. What could this mean?

Material wellbeing
I notice every time I break something that I just throw it out and expect a new one. I don't really look after what I've got.

Psychological wellbeing
What can we learn when we feel down?

Environmental wellbeing
What is nature trying to teach us when we have a problem like climate change?

Cultural wellbeing
How do people feel when they experience racism and discrimination?

Economic wellbeing
I just seem to blow all my money real quick and then get upset I've run out. What's that about?

Where have I been spending my time today?

Practical exercise | Wholeness clock

It's not that you have to engage with all eight components every day. Just monitor where you are dedicating your time and identify where you could invest a bit more. Additionally, it's about recognising when the components become relevant in your daily experiences.

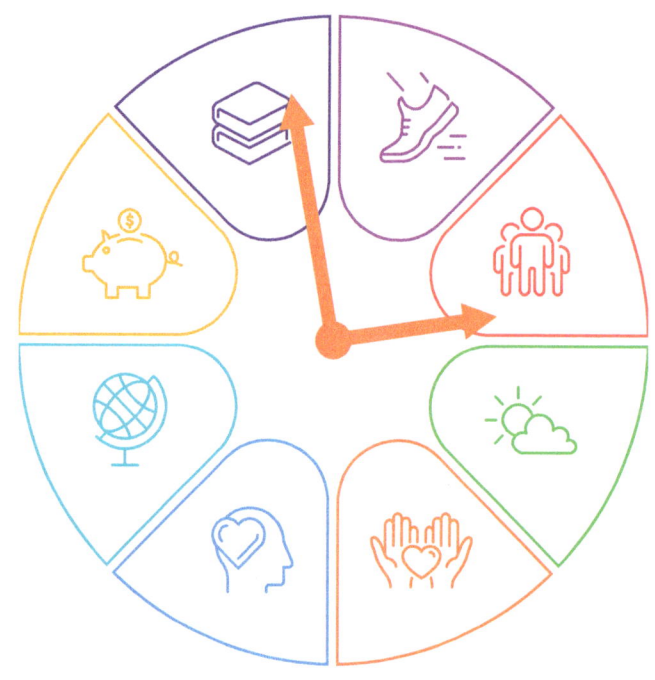

WELLBEING CONVERSATION OPPORTUNITY

The purpose of this exercise is to help us cultivate wellbeing awareness of wholeness as your day is unfolding!

1. Which components of wellbeing have I given attention to today?
2. Which components haven't arisen yet?
3. What opportunities can I create to flow attention and energy to other components?

It's like fitting together a jigsaw

22   Wellbeing Polarity Leadership: How Young Leaders Can Impact the 21st Century

The big switch that **wellbeing polarity leaders make**

 **Learning objective**

In the face of wellbeing tensions, make the big switch from one-sidedness to counter-balance

I do feel a lot better when I work at balance

Our research shows that wellbeing polarity leaders have made a big switch in their thinking.

They have moved from being uncomfortable with contradictions and tensions between wellbeing components to being comfortable and learning to see that contradictions are calling for counter-balance. This is the big switch from one-sidedness to counter-balance.

Jenny is a Grade A student. She studies too hard and has no social life. She feels torn between her studies and friends. She chooses study.

Now, let's delve deeper. Jenny feels 'torn' — a tension between two competing objectives. She makes a decision ('study') and opts for one side over the other. At this point, Jenny is one-sided. In terms of wellbeing, Jenny hasn't honed the skill of counter-balance.

Indeed, Jenny might be overlooking the broader context of why she should even try to counter-balance these two elements. The issue is that while Jenny may be catering to her economic wellbeing (securing a good job in the future), she's compromising her social wellbeing (friendships, connection).

Now, let's examine Jenny's pattern.

The cycle of one-sidedness

As a wellbeing polarity leader, Jenny breaks this cycle. She now values wellbeing and thus questions, 'What is best for my overall wellbeing here?' Jenny recognises a tension and understands that such tensions demand a counter-balance. Although she still feels uneasy, she values this discomfort because she has come to see this tension as an avenue for personal growth. Jenny believes that she needs to study and also maintain a social life. She perceives it this way because she values both her economic and social wellbeing. She is learning to counter-balance.

Now, let's examine Jenny's new cycle.

The cycle of counterbalance

WELLBEING CONVERSATION OPPORTUNITY

Where is my family too one-sided and could use better balance with our wellbeing?

Counter-balance and polarities

Learning objective

Understand the concept of polarities and their energy flows

OK, now we're ready to discuss polarities4. Polarities are a central feature of the wellbeing polarity leadership approach. They're a concept that will assist us in understanding how and why to break and sidestep the cycle of one-sidedness, not only in our personal lives but also in businesses and societies.

Polarities are pairs of opposite positive values that need each other to co-exist. Common examples of polarities include spending versus saving money, studying versus socialising, exercising versus resting, and being an individual versus conforming to a group. Note that each of these pairs represents opposites — there's a tension between spending and saving money; the more we spend, the less we save. Neither of these options is a 'solution' or superior to the other.

When we adopt a one-sided approach, we tend to perceive these as either/or choices — we select one side over the other. However, in doing so, we overlook the importance of both — we disrupt their synergy. To understand this, refer to the subsequent page. The diagram illustrates what's called a polarity map® (Johnson, 2014). This map helps us understand how two elements are interdependent and how energy should circulate freely between them in our lives. Adopting a one-sided perspective can obstruct this energy flow, leading to diminished wellbeing.

So, let's delve into the polarity map®. Grasping this concept will significantly enhance your understanding of yourself and your wellbeing polarity patterns. A polarity map® begins with two poles — elements in tension. These should be two things you genuinely value but which pull you in contrasting directions. In the given example, these are studying and socialising. Following this, the polarity map® is divided into four quadrants. The top two quadrants represent the positive outcomes of focusing on each pole.

The top-left quadrant answers the question: What positive benefits do we derive when we prioritise studying? A potential answer might be achieving the grades necessary to pursue a specific field at uni, leading to a sense of security. The top-right quadrant represents the advantages of socialising, which could encompass feelings of belonging. The map becomes particularly intriguing when we realise that these two elements aren't isolated choices but rather interdependent polarities. The bottom-left quadrant poses a critical question: If we overly concentrate on studying at the expense of socialising, what adverse outcomes might we encounter? We then document our response to this question in the bottom-left quadrant.

---

4 The information we provide here is from three great resources:
Johnson, B. (2014). *Polarity management: Identifying and managing unsolvable problems.* Amherst, MA: HRD Press.
Johnson, B. (2021). *AND: How to leverage polarity/paradox/dilemma.* Amherst, MA: HRD Press.
www.polaritypartnerships.com

5 Each individual writes their own personal answer down.

Polarity map®

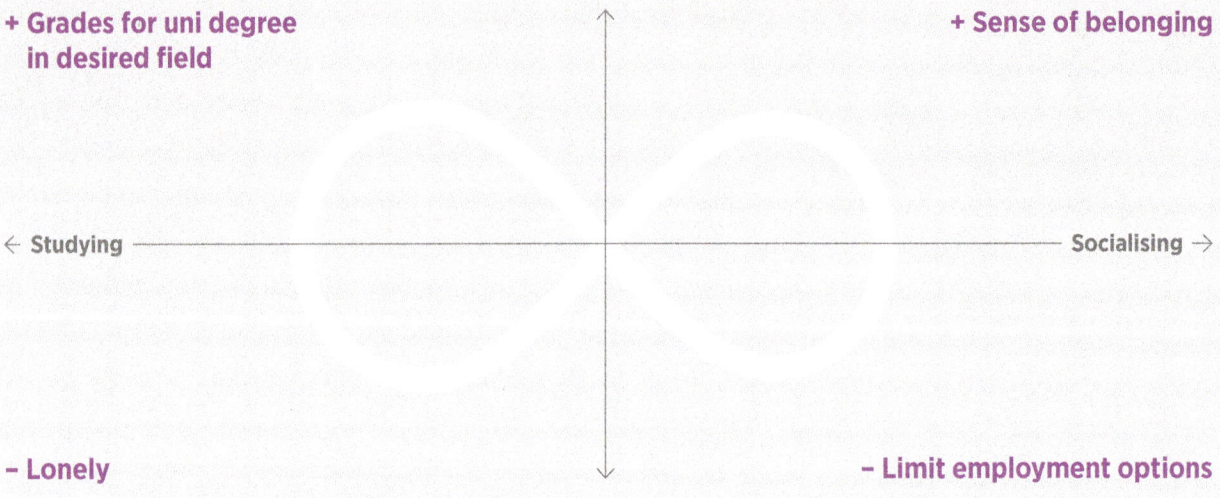

+ Grades for uni degree in desired field

+ Sense of belonging

← Studying

Socialising →

− Lonely

− Limit employment options

The example says that we could feel lonely and isolated. Then the bottom right quadrant asks the question: if we over-focus on socialising to the neglect of studying, what negative result could we experience? We write our answer in the bottom right quadrant. For example, if we spend too much time partying and not enough studying, this may affect the sorts of careers we can apply for and the security and freedom we have in our future life.

Now, the final piece of the polarity map® above is the infinity loop in the middle. The infinity loop is a way of detecting how our energy is flowing between the two poles. When we are one-sided, for instance, we may be spending a lot of time studying and not much time socialising. When this is too much, we may start to feel lonely, and this is a sign that we are not managing this polarity very well. The energy is stalling on the left side, and we are neglecting the right too much.

Now, you may think this is a simple example. OK, so now extend this situation into well-known wellbeing issues confronting our world. Many parents struggle to work **and** invest in family relationships at the same time. Politicians struggle with the idea of how to achieve economic growth **and** environmental sustainability at the same time. And just remember our earlier example of how one-sidedness in a city triggered a negative wellbeing cycle! In each case, our one-sidedness is hurting other aspects of wellbeing. The principles we are teaching here play out in our individual lives but also across all of society. Wellbeing polarity leaders in our research have learnt the valuable lesson of counter-balancing polarities.

Now we're talking: ENERGY!

Counter-balance and polarities

Learning objective

Understand the concept of polarities and their energy flows

OK, now we're ready to discuss polarities4. Polarities are a central feature of the wellbeing polarity leadership approach. They're a concept that will assist us in understanding how and why to break and sidestep the cycle of one-sidedness, not only in our personal lives but also in businesses and societies.

Polarities are pairs of opposite positive values that need each other to co-exist. Common examples of polarities include spending versus saving money, studying versus socialising, exercising versus resting, and being an individual versus conforming to a group. Note that each of these pairs represents opposites — there's a tension between spending and saving money; the more we spend, the less we save. Neither of these options is a 'solution' or superior to the other.

When we adopt a one-sided approach, we tend to perceive these as either/or choices — we select one side over the other. However, in doing so, we overlook the importance of both — we disrupt their synergy. To understand this, refer to the subsequent page. The diagram illustrates what's called a polarity map® (Johnson, 2014). This map helps us understand how two elements are interdependent and how energy should circulate freely between them in our lives. Adopting a one-sided perspective can obstruct this energy flow, leading to diminished wellbeing.

So, let's delve into the polarity map®. Grasping this concept will significantly enhance your understanding of yourself and your wellbeing polarity patterns. A polarity map® begins with two poles — elements in tension. These should be two things you genuinely value but which pull you in contrasting directions. In the given example, these are studying and socialising. Following this, the polarity map® is divided into four quadrants. The top two quadrants represent the positive outcomes of focusing on each pole.

The top-left quadrant answers the question: What positive benefits do we derive when we prioritise studying? A potential answer might be achieving the grades necessary to pursue a specific field at uni, leading to a sense of security. The top-right quadrant represents the advantages of socialising, which could encompass feelings of belonging. The map becomes particularly intriguing when we realise that these two elements aren't isolated choices but rather interdependent polarities. The bottom-left quadrant poses a critical question: If we overly concentrate on studying at the expense of socialising, what adverse outcomes might we encounter? We then document our response to this question in the bottom-left quadrant.

---

4 The information we provide here is from three great resources:
Johnson, B. (2014). *Polarity management: Identifying and managing unsolvable problems*. Amherst, MA: HRD Press.
Johnson, B. (2021). *AND: How to leverage polarity/paradox/dilemma*. Amherst, MA: HRD Press.
www.polaritypartnerships.com

5 Each individual writes their own personal answer down.

Polarity map®

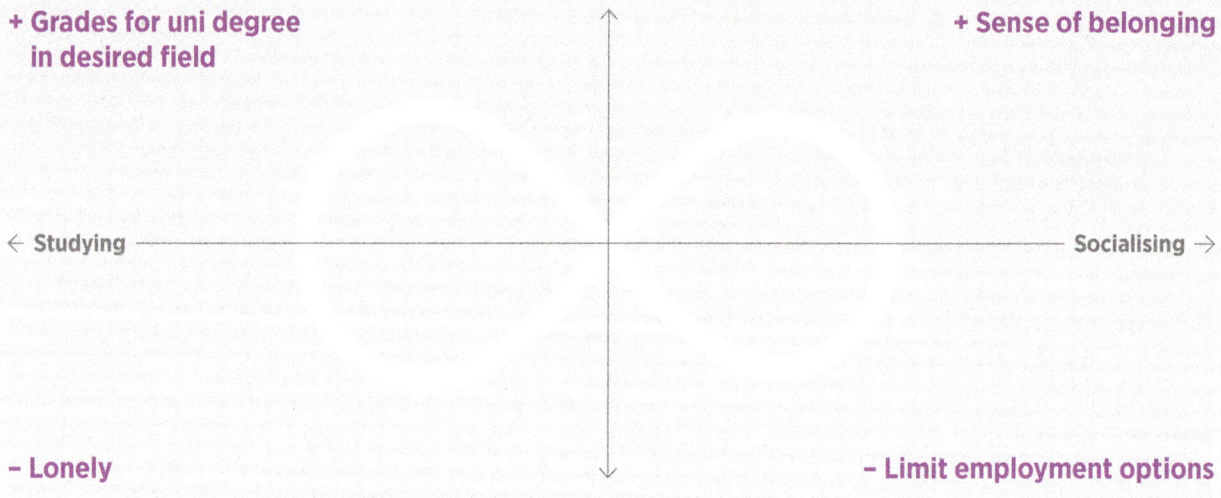

+ Grades for uni degree in desired field　　　　　　　　　　+ Sense of belonging

← Studying　　　　　　　　　　　　　　　　　　　　　　Socialising →

− Lonely　　　　　　　　　　　　　　　　　　　　　　− Limit employment options

The example says that we could feel lonely and isolated. Then the bottom right quadrant asks the question: if we over-focus on socialising to the neglect of studying, what negative result could we experience? We write our answer in the bottom right quadrant. For example, if we spend too much time partying and not enough studying, this may affect the sorts of careers we can apply for and the security and freedom we have in our future life.

Now, the final piece of the polarity map® above is the infinity loop in the middle. The infinity loop is a way of detecting how our energy is flowing between the two poles. When we are one-sided, for instance, we may be spending a lot of time studying and not much time socialising. When this is too much, we may start to feel lonely, and this is a sign that we are not managing this polarity very well. The energy is stalling on the left side, and we are neglecting the right too much.

Now, you may think this is a simple example. OK, so now extend this situation into well-known wellbeing issues confronting our world. Many parents struggle to work **and** invest in family relationships at the same time. Politicians struggle with the idea of how to achieve economic growth **and** environmental sustainability at the same time. And just remember our earlier example of how one-sidedness in a city triggered a negative wellbeing cycle! In each case, our one-sidedness is hurting other aspects of wellbeing. The principles we are teaching here play out in our individual lives but also across all of society. Wellbeing polarity leaders in our research have learnt the valuable lesson of counter-balancing polarities.

Now we're talking: ENERGY!

How one-sidedness affects everything

The tables below show how one-sidedness can affect individuals, businesses and societies.

What we learn is that one-sidedness is a perspective that we take into all areas of our lives. This means that we keep creating unnecessary harm—one-sidedness costs individuals, businesses and societies. The answer is to re-connect the polarity which our one-sidedness has torn apart. We need to think differently and make connecting opposites and polarities our new normal. Then we will break negative wellbeing cycles in individual lives but also in our businesses and societies.

Personal one-sidedness…	Polarities we are avoiding…
When we want just peace and happiness and a life free of turmoil ('I wish all my troubles would just go away').	That peace is the acceptance of turmoil. **Both** happiness **and** turmoil have their place.
When we always want things done our way	Having independence also requires interdependence. **Both** independence **and** interdependence have their place.
I like structure, order and being in control. I hate it when things get chaotic	**Both** structure **and** flexibility have their place.

Business one-sidedness…	Polarities we are avoiding…
We exist to create value for shareholders first and foremost	Creating value for shareholders also requires creating value for stakeholders (employees, natural environment, suppliers, government) at the same time.
Let's focus on making money and worry about the natural environment later.	Growing money and regenerating the environment at the same time. Making money depends on the health of the natural environment. **Both** money **and** the natural environment at the same time.
Let's just stick to what we do best	Surviving today also requires looking after tomorrow. **Both** stay same **and** change at the same time.

Society one-sidedness…	Polarities we are avoiding…
Societies run best when everybody pursues their own self-interest	Community-interest is also self-interest. **Both** self **and** community at the same time.
The richer we get the better our life will be	To gain life you also have to lose it. Spirituality can emphasize not basing your life satisfaction on external things. **Both** material things **and** spiritual at the same time.
Societies should stick to tradition and the way we've always done things	Long-term survival requires stability and change. **Both** tradition **and** change.

The link between wholeness and polarities

 **Learning objective**

Understand the link between the concepts of wholeness and polarities for wellbeing leadership

Now that we have covered both wholeness and polarities, a key insight emerges: how we manage our polarities within and across all eight of the components is important to our wellbeing. It's also important to our societies!

Wholeness is about bringing all eight components of wellbeing together, while polarities are about **how** we bring them together and **keep** them together on a day-to-day basis. So, when we have wellbeing issues in our life, we can ask:

1. What components of wellbeing are involved?
2. Where am I being one-sided and not looking after a polarity very well?
3. How can I do better at making sure I'm investing enough in both sides of a wellbeing polarity?

Note that looking after a polarity does not mean an equal balance of attention on both poles. It's about finding the right amount to invest in each that avoids excessive time spent experiencing the bottom left quadrants. The key to wellbeing is not the equal balance—it's managing the infinity loop of energy in a way that makes sure you are experiencing more of the positive benefits in the two upper quadrants and the least time experiencing either of the bottom two quadrants (signs of becoming too one-sided).

It feels a lot like dancing to me

Practical

Building wellbeing polarity **leadership competency**

How's my within-component counterbalance?

Beginners | **Wellbeing polarity leadership competency 1**

🎯 **Learning objective**

Become aware of the polarities (tensions) that can arise in your life and that need counter-balancing *within* each component

I love being more aware of the eight.

The beginner pathway

1	Introduce young emerging leaders to each of the eight components
2	Explain that wellbeing requires balancing polarities within components
3	Discuss the wellbeing polarities or other ones you see/experience within components
4	Discuss wellbeing issues
5	Encourage awareness of components and counter-balancing polarities within
6	Encourage flow between **both** sides of a polarity
7	Reflect on your experiences

Balancing **within components**

Getting comfortable with polarities

EARLY WARNING SIGNS OF IMBALANCE/ONE-SIDEDNESS

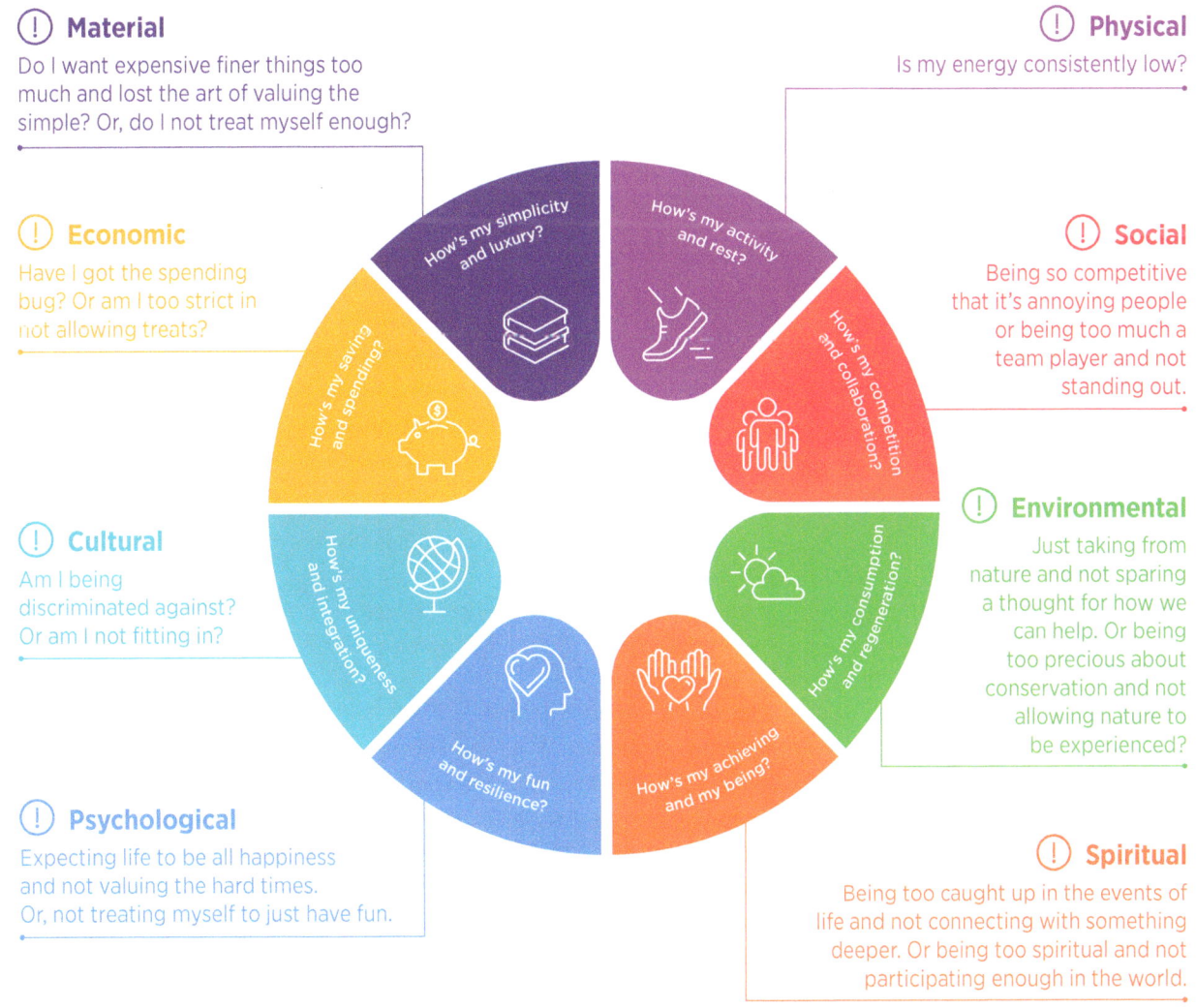

⚠ **Material**
Do I want expensive finer things too much and lost the art of valuing the simple? Or, do I not treat myself enough?

⚠ **Economic**
Have I got the spending bug? Or am I too strict in not allowing treats?

⚠ **Cultural**
Am I being discriminated against? Or am I not fitting in?

⚠ **Psychological**
Expecting life to be all happiness and not valuing the hard times. Or, not treating myself to just have fun.

⚠ **Physical**
Is my energy consistently low?

⚠ **Social**
Being so competitive that it's annoying people or being too much a team player and not standing out.

⚠ **Environmental**
Just taking from nature and not sparing a thought for how we can help. Or being too precious about conservation and not allowing nature to be experienced?

⚠ **Spiritual**
Being too caught up in the events of life and not connecting with something deeper. Or being too spiritual and not participating enough in the world.

Valuing our polarities

The questions explained

Economic wellbeing—
How's my saving and spending?

Economic wellbeing involves a tension between keeping some money for a rainy day but also making sure we allow ourselves the things money can buy.

Environmental wellbeing—
How's my consumption and regeneration?

Nature provides us many things to enjoy including beaches, oceans, food, trees and grass. But if all we do is treat these things by using them then we aren't looking after them. That's not a healthy relationship with nature. So, we need to balance our using with regenerating—doing the things that allow nature to live healthily.

Physical wellbeing—
How's my activity and rest?

Sometimes we push ourselves too much for too long. Or sometimes we get lazy and don't push ourselves enough. Learn to get the flow between activity and rest and not too much of one or the other.

Psychological wellbeing—
How's my fun and resilience?

We all want to be happy and enjoy ourselves, but sometimes we expect life to be all ups and no downs. That's not how it is. The downs can be important teachers about wellbeing. So, we need to have our fun, but also recognise that the difficult times also are needed to help us grow.

Material wellbeing—
How's my simplicity and luxury?

We all know it: we love to buy stuff. But we can get caught in the trap of thinking we always need to be in luxury and forget how to enjoy the simple things in life.

Spiritual wellbeing—
How's my achieving and my being?

Spiritual wisdom has long taught that we need to learn to live in the world but also learn an inner contentment that doesn't get caught up in the ups and downs of the world. Somewhere along the way we have lost this wisdom, leaving ourselves and our Young Emerging Leaders not able to see more deeply.

Being is a state of mindfulness which places no expectations on self or world and how they should be. It is an attitude of acceptance as is.

Social wellbeing—
How's my competition and collaboration?

Social wellbeing is about how we connect with other people. Sometimes we get too caught up in trying to be the best and forget how to work with other people. Or, we are a real team player but don't develop how we stand out.

Cultural wellbeing—
How's my uniqueness and integration?

Sometimes we expect everyone to be the same and don't value difference. Other times we may be too focused on what makes us different that we keep to ourselves too much and don't mix.

WELLBEING CONVERSATION OPPORTUNITY

The tool is meant to be a conversation piece between parents/caregivers and Young Emerging Leaders. As problems present for parents/caregivers or Young Emerging Leaders then use the tool to help diagnose the issue and point to a better wellbeing direction—have you got a problem of wholeness, counterbalance or both?

This is not so much about scoring yourself as it is about moment-to-moment awareness and the ability to flow.

How's my across-component counterbalance?

Advanced | Wellbeing polarity leadership competency 2

 **Learning objective**

Become aware of the polarities that can arise in your life and that need counter-balancing across opposite pairs of components

Once you've got some experience at practicing your within-component counter-balance then see if you can now add one more competency: understanding how to get two components to counter-balance each other.

OK, you're testing me now but I think I've got this

The advanced pathway

1	Explain that wellbeing requires balancing polarities across components
2	Discuss across-component polarities or other ones you see/experience
3	Discuss Issues
4	Encourage awareness of counter-balancing opposite components
5	Encourage flow

Balancing across components

Getting comfortable with polarities

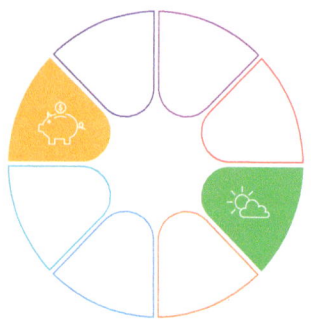

Economic and environmental wellbeing example polarity

How's my purchasing **and** looking after the natural environment at the same time?

Cultural and social wellbeing example polarity

How can I respect diversity and be part of a larger group at the same time? (We are one but we are many)

Material and spiritual wellbeing example polarity

How's my focus on the things that change in the world **and** my focus on the eternal?

Psychological and physical wellbeing example polarity

How am I balancing thinking **and** doing, theory **and** practice, knowledge **and** skills, reflection and action?

WELLBEING CONVERSATION OPPORTUNITY

These are not the only opposite pairs that may show up in your life. Just try to practice recognising when two components of wellbeing are pulling you in opposite directions. Be comfortable with that and say 'OK, I need to counter-balance here'.

The questions we pose in each example above are also just examples. There may be other ways in your life the wellbeing components come into tension and conflict. Just remember, tension and conflict are OK. In fact, it's good. It's just our usual reaction is to choose one or the other instead of thinking 'counter-balance'. If we make the switch from being uncomfortable with tension and choosing one or the other side over to liking the tension and choosing both, then we have made the big switch towards wellbeing polarity leadership.

Wellbeing leadership **in action**

Getting practical—mega-advanced section!
Wellbeing polarity leadership competency 3

OK, so how can leaders actually use wellbeing polarity leadership in the workplace? And how would it lead to better results?

To answer this, we need to go back to the different types of problem that leaders face—technical and adaptive. Each of these different types of problems can use the wellbeing wheel in different ways. But the overall benefit is to ensure that the decisions that leaders make enhance and not harm wellbeing across the components in the wheel.

Leaders can:

1. Connect their technical solutions to technical problems with the wellbeing wheel;
2. Identify adaptive problems that require a wellbeing polarity approach;
3. Connect technical problems with adaptive problems and use a combination of approaches.

Here is a decision aid to illustrate these choices:

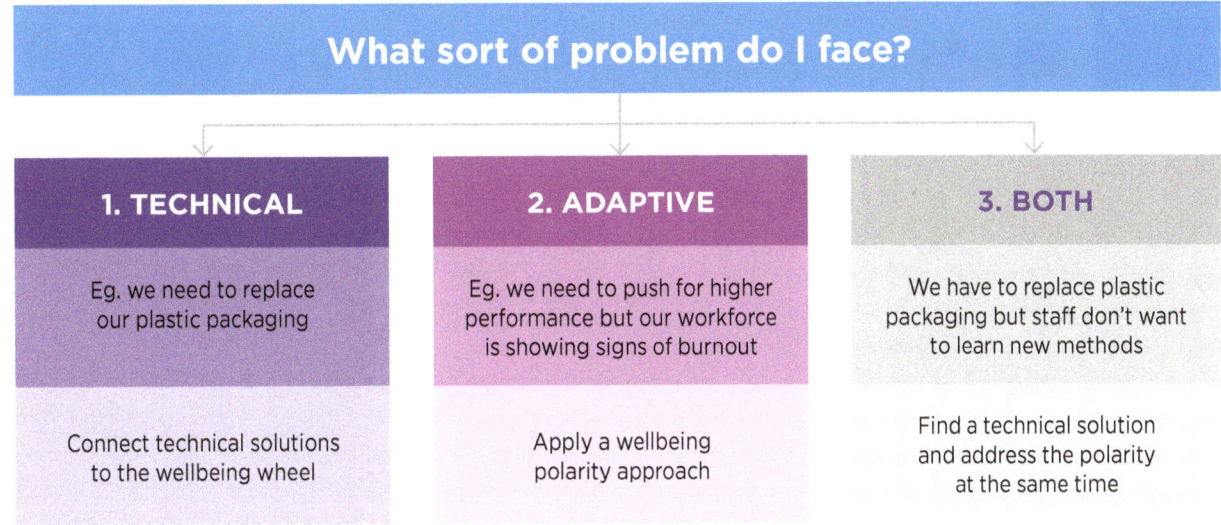

Back to technical and adaptive **challenges**

 **Learning objective**

Understand the difference between technical and wellbeing layers of jobs

So let's now connect wellbeing with our earlier distinction between technical and adaptive problems. Then we will really begin to see how the leadership game has changed in terms of wellbeing.

When leaders go about their work, they can often be focused on the technical aspects of the job: what tasks do we need to complete? What are our performance goals? What expert knowledge must we apply? What staff issues are we facing? And so on. While leaders are often trained in specialist knowledge, they also gather on-the-job experience and gain knowledge about how to work in a specific organisation.

The figure below illustrates how Embracers not only concentrate on the technical aspects of the job but also recognise an additional layer around it—the wellbeing context. Some of the challenges they encounter are technical and demand technical solutions, e.g., how will we expand our business? However, Embracers aim to achieve these technical objectives while simultaneously promoting (not harming) wellbeing.

When faced with situations at work, Embracers ponder: Can this issue bridge both the technical and wellbeing layers? By implementing this technical solution, might I jeopardise wellbeing? Whenever possible, the goal is to have the technical facets of a job serve a loftier purpose of enhancing wellbeing.

The wellbeing insights you gain from this book enhance your awareness of these two layers:

1. Being technically competent in required tasks, **and**
2. Executing technical tasks in a manner that also fosters wellbeing for all involved.

Embracers excel in both areas, and we can educate a new generation of leaders to intertwine their technical prowess with wellbeing outcomes.

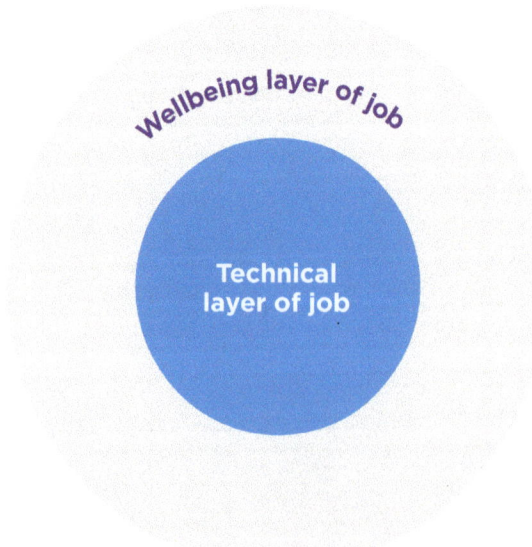

WELLBEING CONVERSATION OPPORTUNITY

Where can my school or workplace do better at connecting technical tasks with wellbeing?

Situation 1
TECHNICAL PROBLEMS

Connect technical solutions to the wellbeing wheel

Technical problems arise when you encounter a challenge that can be addressed using your technical expertise. However, we learned a crucial lesson with plastic packaging. Large companies faced a technical challenge in finding an affordable and convenient way to package their products. Plastic emerged as the solution—it was inexpensive, convenient, and readily available. Thus, the technical problem was addressed. Yet, we discovered that, once discarded, plastic causes significant harm to the natural environment, including our world's oceans.

What we recognise is that it's insufficient to merely devise solutions to technical problems without also considering the wellbeing wheel. While plastic certainly satisfied the economic wellbeing criterion for companies, it failed in the environmental wellbeing aspect. The wellbeing wheel provides leaders with a framework to ensure that when developing technical solutions, they can comprehensively assess the wellbeing implications. Nature has imparted this invaluable lesson to us!

 Lesson learned

That technical problems and solutions have wellbeing impacts.

 Risk

Developing technical solutions without considering impacts on wellbeing components.

Situation 2
ADAPTIVE PROBLEMS

Apply a wellbeing polarity approach

Adaptive problems arise when you're faced with a situation that pulls you in opposite directions. The aforementioned Situation 2 exemplifies such a predicament. It's a frequent tension/conflict that leaders encounter: the organisation needs to bolster its performance, yet the workforce is fatigued. These situations don't merely require a technical solution. Instead, leaders would fare better treating these challenges as adaptive problems—a tug-of-war between performance and wellbeing. Rather than reacting hastily to find a solution, such as granting workers a break, leaders should also inquire, 'How did we land in this predicament to begin with?' This is where a focus on polarity becomes crucial.

We likely found ourselves in this bind because we incessantly emphasised performance, overlooking the mental and physical health of our staff. The scale has tipped excessively towards performance. This presents an inherent tension: while we need to perform, our mental and physical capacities set boundaries. Thus, we're confronted with a polarity between performance and wellbeing. Yet, we've been lopsided, highlighting performance while neglecting wellbeing. Within the framework of the wellbeing wheel, this can manifest as a polarity between economic wellbeing (performance) and both physical and psychological wellbeing. While this may seem evident, our research indicates that many leaders don't contemplate these polarities, rendering their workplaces susceptible to the very challenges we're discussing. The wellbeing polarity wheel equips leaders to sidestep the considerable human toll of staff burnout. Not only are the employees affected, but their families and the performance of their organisations also bear the brunt. Nature imparts yet another vital lesson: performance is pivotal, but not at the expense of our health! Our wellbeing compels us to reevaluate our disproportionate emphasis on performance.

 Lesson learned

That adaptive problems involve wellbeing tensions that need counter-balancing.

 Risk

Choosing one side of the tension.

Embracers concentrate on the technical aspects of the job but also see another layer around this—the wellbeing context.

Some of the problems they face will be technical in nature and require technical solutions but Embracers aim to achieve these technical goals and create (not harm) wellbeing at the same time.

Situation 3
TECHNICAL AND ADAPTIVE PROBLEMS AT SAME TIME

Find a technical solution and address the polarity at the same time

Technical and adaptive problems can arise simultaneously when both a technical solution and a wellbeing polarity are evident. This is reflected in Situation 3 above and necessitates leaders to distinguish between the technical and adaptive challenges. Firstly, we need to identify a substitute for plastic that aligns with our criteria on the wellbeing wheel. Moreover, our staff are hesitant to adopt a new method, primarily because they're experiencing burnout. Thus, we must seek both a technical solution and an adaptive response concurrently. We can formulate a technical solution drawing upon our scientific expertise and by assessing various alternatives in light of their effects on the wellbeing wheel. Concurrently, we must adopt a polarity perspective, striving to achieve a balance between performance and wellbeing.

 Lesson learned

That technical and adaptive problems call for different ways of working with wellbeing.

 Risk

Developing technical solutions without also addressing underlying adaptive problems which involve a poorly-leveraged polarity.

I'll look for opportunities to link both technical and wellbeing layers

38 Wellbeing Polarity Leadership: How Young Leaders Can Impact the 21st Century

Personal development

Help for making your **personal leadership changes**

The process of **inner change**

 **Learning objective**

Understand the process of inner change

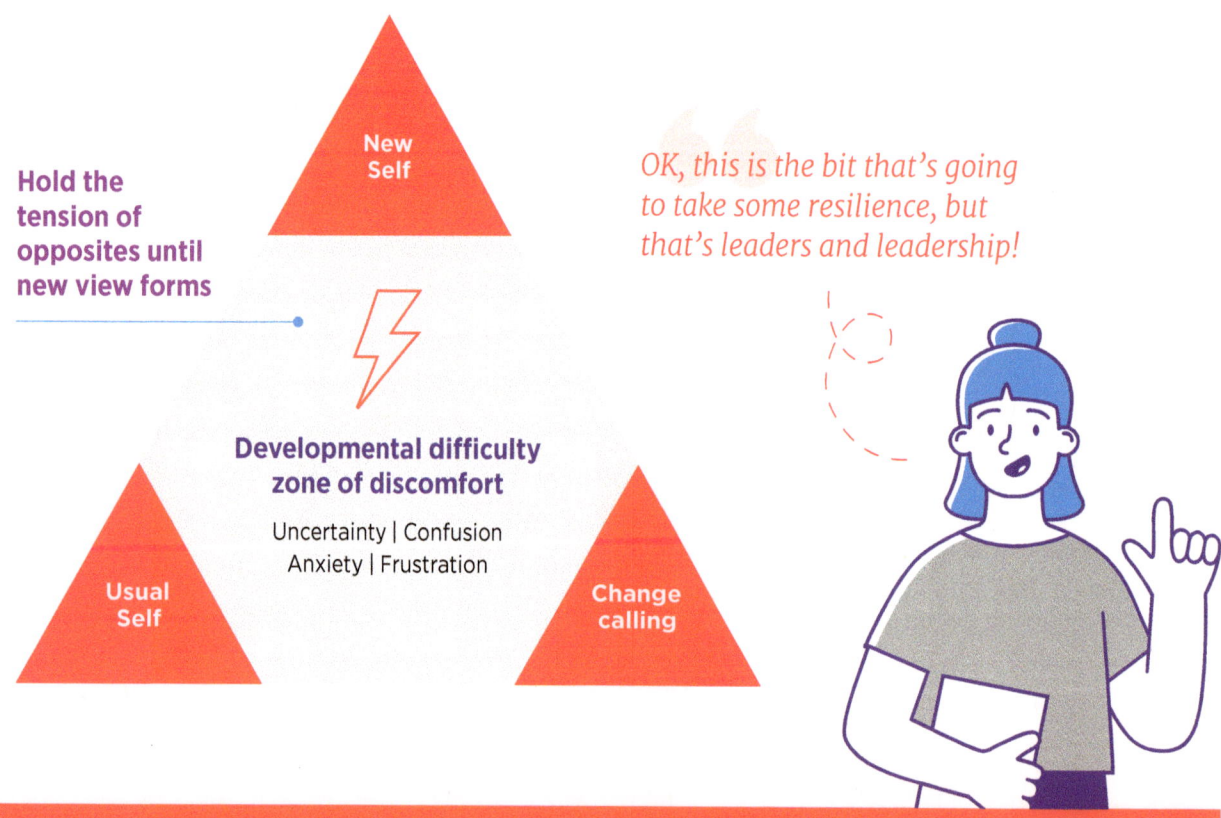

OK, this is the bit that's going to take some resilience, but that's leaders and leadership!

Self transformation—the process of inner change

Adult developmental psychology observes that the process of inner change works like a triangle. There is your usual self that is disrupted by a developmental difficulty—a tough situation that is challenging how you look at self, others and the world. Then an inner tension occurs—you become caught between your usual self and the need to add in some new change.

But change is hard and becomes a battle in your mind between your usual self and the call to change.

At this stage, you may feel uncertain about whether to change or not and/or what exactly the change is that you need. You may feel confused between these two sides. This battle, although uncomfortable, is normal and a good thing. This is called 'holding the tension of opposites'. It is at this point most people give up. Their inner dragon has won (see next page). Those who grow (the hero within) stay with the tension until they find a new way that finds a blend between the usual self and the new change. Eventually a new you is born.

Hero and **the dragon**

Resistance to change—when you just can't be bothered versus stepping into your strength

 Learning objective

Learn that resistance to change involves a battle between a hero and a dragon

Have you heard of those ancient myths about a hero and a dragon battling it out? This is an age-old tale of how as soon as we embark on a new path there is an equal resistance pulling us back to our old self.

So, in those moments, we can either choose to go in the direction of growth or shrink back to our comfort zone of complacency. The hero is the new self wanting to be born—a wellbeing polarity leader. The dragon is your old self pulling you back to stay as you are. The dragon is also that part of you that pulls you back into being lazy and not trying. The dragon will say all sorts of things to you to stop you from growing. Recognise the dragon's voice and work through the resistance. Maybe the dragon doubts that this wellbeing stuff is worth it. Maybe it questions whether you really need it.

When you give in to the thoughts of the dragon you feed it and it grows. That becomes you...it devours you! But the more you starve the dragon and feed your hero who wants to grow and conquer then that will become you. Becoming a wellbeing polarity leader requires you to feed this new hero and starve the dragon. Do you notice that there is a new contradiction for you to master: feed and starve at the same time! Slowly but surely let your hero win the battle and allow you to grow.

Recognise the respective voices of the hero and dragon

VOICE OF THE HERO WITHIN

VOICE OF THE DRAGON WITHIN

← Grow   Shrink →

'Go for your true potential'

'Don't get stuck in limiting beliefs and patterns'

'Change is hard but that is the hero's journey'

'You don't need to change'

'Stay as you are'

'All this growth stuff is nonsense'

'You're doing just fine the way you are'

'This is all too hard. Just go back to bed'

Getting your hero on

CHANGING OUR THINKING— THE POWER OF A 'HOW MIGHT WE' QUESTION AND A 'GROWTH MINDSET'

Often, we encounter problem statements on various levels: personal, community, governmental, and global. Consider the following statements:

'The movies are too expensive to attend.'

'There is too much rubbish littering the local park.'

'There are more homeless people living on the streets.'

'Deforestation is impacting climate change.'

No matter the problem, converting the statement into a question helps reframe our thinking and directs our efforts from stating problems to suggesting solutions. The 'how might we' format shifts our perspective: 'how' suggests strategy development, 'might' introduces potential, and 'we' signifies collective effort.

For example:

'The movies are too expensive to attend.'

'How might we afford to attend the movies?'

'There is too much rubbish littering the local park.'

'How might we clean up the local park?'

'There are more homeless people living on the streets.'

'How might we support homeless individuals?'

'Deforestation is impacting climate change.'

'How might we halt deforestation and its effects on climate change?'

While the challenges remain formidable, framing them as questions fosters collaboration, innovative thinking, and novel approaches. This shift in mindset, however, doesn't negate that some issues demand significant time and effort for even marginal positive change. Adopting a growth mindset, as presented by Carol Dweck in Mindset: The New Psychology of Success, can bolster our persistence, resilience, and dedication to our goals. Sometimes, merely appending the word 'yet' can profoundly alter our perception and aspiration.

For instance:

Katy observed excessive litter in the local park, a favourite family hangout. Recently, hazards like broken glass on the paths, bottles and cans strewn about, and used syringes in public toilets marred the park's appeal. Discussing her concerns with her father, Katy lamented, 'There's too much rubbish littering the local park.' This conversation led them to rephrase the problem: 'How might we clean up the local park?'

Motivated to make a change, Katy listed potential volunteers and, with her father's help, designed a poster advertising a park cleanup day. The local council not only supplied cleanup materials but also promptly attended to the hazardous litter. Though the park's condition improved, Katy still felt it wasn't up to par. Her father optimistically added, '…yet.'

On the cleanup day, over 50 community members joined the effort, including local businesses. Three hours later, the transformation was astonishing. Katy was inspired to organise monthly cleanups and was elated to see their ripple effect: reduced litter, increased park usage, and a new playground funded by the council and local businesses. Katy's initial efforts yielded results beyond her wildest expectations.

My coach says 'our biggest enemy is ourselves'

Practical exercise

Reflection on **experience**

What new benefits have entered my life as a result of working with the wellbeing polarity wheel?

What am I finding difficult with my wellbeing polarity wheel experience?

How does my hero/dragon battle show up? Where do I lose motivation? Why? What works to get me focused again?

What questions do I have?

Frequently asked **questions**

Do I really need all eight components? For example, I'm not into that spiritual stuff.

Many people live their lives without considering all eight components. See each component as latent potential. It's an inherent possibility within us, and it's our choice to activate that potential and reap its benefits. Sometimes, challenging periods might indicate a neglected aspect of our lives. These symptoms might be nudging you to tap into an untapped potential.

How can I possibly think about all eight? I've got enough on my plate. Isn't that a bitmuch?

Our research indicates that issues related to the eight components are always around us; we're just not always conscious of them. Often, our decisions influence these eight aspects; it's about heightening our awareness and intentionally engaging with the model. If it resonates, you'll naturally be inclined to integrate it more. You don't need to ponder this constantly. Live your life, and simply be aware when facets of wellbeing, wholeness, or counterbalance surface in your experiences. Reflect: are you neglecting a wellbeing aspect? Are you stuck, failing to balance contrasting elements? Are you biased on an issue that should be viewed as a wellbeing tension requiring a balanced perspective?

Are you suggesting I become religious?

No, we're not preaching any doctrine here. Each individual must embark on their personal journey of discovery to discern what resonates within each component. The spiritual component invites exploration—its interpretation is subjective. Yet, remember its role in holistic unity. The spiritual element can offer equilibrium if there's excessive materialism or if you're overly self-centric without acknowledging deeper realms. Delve into what 'spiritual' means for you—it might be religious or perhaps not. And remember, your interpretations might evolve over time.

Wellbeing Polarity Wheel: Becoming a

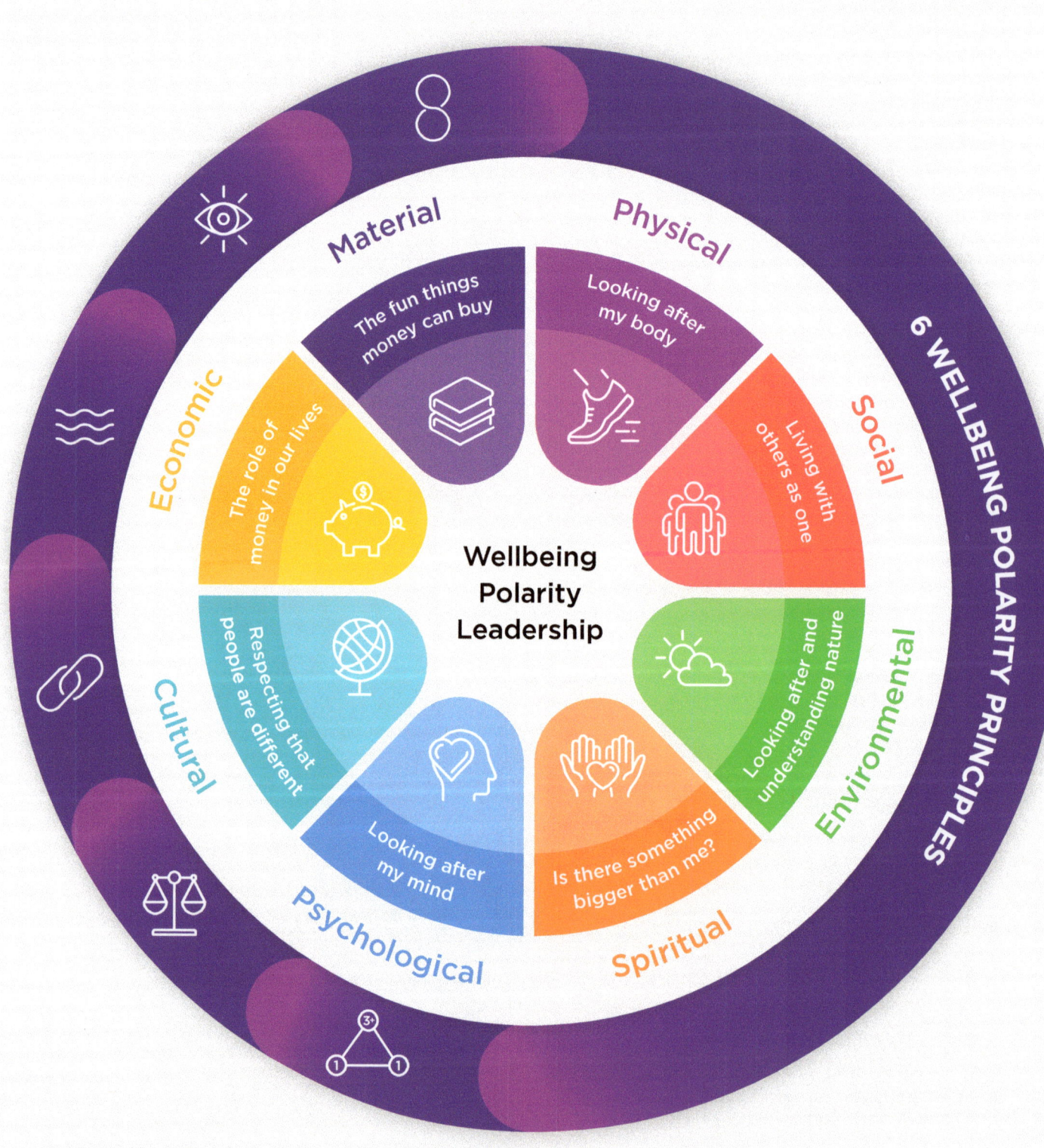

21st Century Wellbeing Leader

Wholeness
Include the *eight*, mate
Am I looking after all eight?

Awareness
Open your eyes, guys
As issues arise do I know what wellbeing components are at play?

Flow
Go with the *flow*, Jo
Whoops, which components do I tend to forget? Where do I get stuck doing too much of one component and not enough of others?

Link
Build a *bridge*, Ridge
How can I do two at once?

Balance
Can you *balance*?
How is my see-saw going?

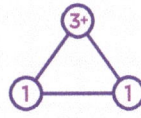
Synergise
Go *higher*, Jemima
If I do both of these at the same time, what can I create?

Revised who am I?

OK, so do you remember doing the Who am I? exercise back at the start of this book? Well, we sure have been on an adventure working through all this new wellbeing polarity leadership material.

It would be really interesting now to see how you have changed as a result of doing this work. Here is a list of questions to ponder to see how you have changed:

1. What do you think wellbeing is? How has your understanding changed from the beginning of the Wellbeing Polarity Leadership content?

2. What do you think a leader is? What do you think makes a good leader?

3. Do you consider yourself a leader now?

4. Where in your life can you observe two opposite but positive values (polarities) that you're trying to balance? For example, prioritising study AND social relationships. Balancing physical **and** online connection with others.

5. What wellbeing polarity conversations have you engaged in since learning about the concepts?

6. How has your way of approaching/language used to approach difficult conversations changed?

7. What is a situation where you have implemented the wellbeing polarity wheel framework/theory to thrive resiliently when faced with a challenge? For example...

8. What have you learnt about yourself through engaging in the Wellbeing Polarity Leadership content?

Appendix

Practical exercises for building our competencies **in the components of wellbeing**

Economic wellbeing

Claim—every person is entitled to make as much money as they can and build wealth without having to pay taxes or contribute to the financial aid of others.

Activity—compass points[6]

Read the claim and complete each part of the reflection.
N—Need | S—Stance or suggestions | E—Exciting | W—Worrisome

What else do I need to know or understand about this claim?

What do I find worrisome about this idea? What is the downside?

What excites me about this claim? What is the upside to this type of thinking?

What is my current stance on this issue? What suggestions can I put forward?

---

[6] This activity has been adapted using the ideas behind The Compass Points thinking routine that was developed by Project Zero, a research centre at the Harvard Graduate School of Education.

Cultural **wellbeing**

We strive to compete, to enjoy and to survive. Today, we have access to a multitude of products and luxuries. The question is, do we really need everything we have or desire to have?

Activity 1—see, think, wonder[7]. Analyse the pictures:

	See (who, what, where)	Think (what do I know?)	Wonder (what questions do I have?)

Activity 2—why is cultural wellbeing important?

Extension discussion

I want to make more friends but I don't understand the other person's beliefs.

---

[7] This activity has been adapted using the ideas behind The See, Think, Wonder thinking routine that was developed by Project Zero, a research centre at the Harvard Graduate School of Education.

Environmental **wellbeing**

For each given claim, find evidence to support it. Add a question to prompt your thinking about how you might make a difference. The first is an example. Visit sdgs.un.org/goals for research.

Claim[8]	Evidence to support	Opportunities
The environment must not be sacrificed to create homes and businesses.	In the past two decades, the world has lost 100 million hectares of forest.	How might we encourage businesses and governments to build up rather than out?
Coral are not important to life on Earth.		
There is more than enough resources to feed, clothe, and shelter more than 7 billion people on Earth.		
There is no such thing as 'clean energy.'		
Dead Zones in the ocean do not exist.		
Climate change is a myth.		

[8] This activity has been adapted using the ideas behind The Claim, Support, Question thinking routine that was developed by Project Zero, a research centre at the Harvard Graduate School of Education.

Material **wellbeing**

We strive to compete, to enjoy and to survive. Today, we have access to a multitude of products and luxuries. The question is, do we really need everything we have or desire to have?

A mental 'tug of war'[9]

For each item listed below, consider carefully if the item is a need or want. A need is something you cannot survive without. A want may make life easier or more comfortable.

Item	Need	Want
Water	○	○
Smartphone	○	○
Friends	○	○
Shelter	○	○

Reflect

What do I really need? What do I value? Are there other aspects to my wellbeing that play a part in my thinking?

E.g. My phone can text and call but do I need all the features of a latest model smartphone? What do I need? Is this worth my energy and money? Add your ideas below.

---

[9] This activity has been adapted using the ideas behind The Tug of War thinking routine that was developed by Project Zero, a research centre at the Harvard Graduate School of Education

Physical **wellbeing**

How are you tracking? Being mindful of our body and the signals it gives us is an essential part of our overall wellbeing. Sometimes, it is worthwhile to reflect on our ability to listen to our body and review our habits and routines.

How well are you tracking?

Keep a movement diary for one week. Are you moving enough? Are you sleeping so that you receive the rest required to make good decisions or achieve your peak performance?

Activity/day	1	2	3	4	5	6	7
Hours/minutes sleeping							
Activity 1							
Activity 2							
Activity 3							
Activity 4							

Reflect

**Is there a balance between the types of activities you do? Moving versus resting.
Are you getting enough quality sleep or movement in your day?
What could you change to take better care of your physical wellbeing?**

_____
_____
_____
_____
_____
_____

Social **wellbeing**

There are times when we need to change our perspective and our interactions with others. A balance is required between competition, humility, striving for personal best, and allowing others to thrive with our support.

Over the picture below, add your thoughts about people and teams. What are the parts of a team? How do teams behave? Which perspectives can you look at teams from? How are you involved or how do you contribute? How do we achieve awesomeness for ourselves and the group?

Reflect

What actions can you take in your life to support the teams you are a part of whilst still ensuring your own success?

_____

_____

_____

_____

Psychological **wellbeing**

We all want to thrive. It's important to 'notice' the positive actions we take to care for ourselves and those around us, and to make a positive difference. Think about the past week — have there been moments when you've faced challenges, made a difference, or supported someone else? Reflect below.

Experience/ideas	Who was involved?	The context	How I felt about this experience
A time when I have struggled			
A time when I have made a difference			
A time when I have supported another person			

List three ways that you can tell when you have made a positive difference in the life of another person.

1.

2.

3.

List five people who you can rely upon to support you when you are experiencing a struggle.

1.

2.

3.

4.

5.

Spiritual **wellbeing**

Where and to what do I belong? This activity is designed in two parts to be completed over a couple of weeks. Remember: spiritual wellbeing isn't necessarily about religion; it's about our inner thoughts regarding the world and our place within it.

A bridge in my thinking[10]

List the groups to which you belong below. Consider why you are part of these groups and the support they provide you. First, complete Part 1 of the table below. After waiting at least two weeks, proceed to complete Part 2.

	Words or ideas	Questions	Metaphor or simile
Part 1			
Part 2			

Words or ideas—list how you feel about belonging to your groups.
Questions—write two questions that you have about belonging.
Write a metaphor or similar that best describes your feelings about belonging.

Reflect

There are reasons why humans, just like all animals, need groups. Groups help us to learn, to shape our behaviour, to feel connected, and to help us succeed and achieve. Our belonging to groups, helps to remind us about the importance of inner contentment. Being part of a group allows us the freedom to be less egocentric and more global in our thinking. Groups ground us and give us the opportunity to be mindful. What have you learnt from your belonging to various groups?

---

[10] This activity has been adapted using the ideas behind The 3-2-1 Bridge thinking routine that was developed by Project Zero, a research centre at the Harvard Graduate School of Education

Spiritual wellbeing

Spiritual wellbeing plays a specific role in the counter-balancing set of wellbeing components. But 'spiritual' has become poorly understood and maligned in our society. Spiritual is regarded as 'unscientific', 'irrational', equivalent to believing in Santa Claus.

This perspective isn't the right way to approach 'spiritual'. Spiritual invites a deeper way of seeing and existing in our lives. The major religions have long recognised the importance of nurturing our spiritual facets. While science aids in understanding the physical world, 'spiritual' delves beyond the tangible to explore other layers of reality.

To comprehend the role of spiritual within the wellbeing components, it's beneficial to define it in contrast to its counterpart: 'material' wellbeing. Material wellbeing revolves around prospering in terms of possessions and tangible assets. However, like all other components, if we become overly invested in materialistic pursuits, we risk feeling unfulfilled in their absence. Moreover, we miss out on embracing an entirely different mode of experiencing the world.

The table below juxtaposes material and spiritual wellbeing. If the spiritual wellbeing column seems unfamiliar or odd, it might indicate an excessive emphasis on a materialistic worldview. Cultivating a spiritual mindset can offer immense comfort and fortitude in our lives.

Material	Spiritual
Things money can buy outside yourself	Owned inside
Identify with your worldly persona/role	Free of identifications
Grasping at wanting things a certain way	Flowing, accepting things as they arise
Definable boundaries and properties	Can't be contained as a concept with boundaries
Identified with achievements and possessions in the world	Free of identifications
Ups and downs of life	Transcends the ups and downs
Caught in time and space	Eternal
Grounded in science	Approached through symbolism and mythology

Remember, 'material' pertains to tangible things, whereas spiritual concerns the intangible. Consider the term 'spirit' — a spirit is free, boundless, and cannot be easily defined as a mere concept. In our world, we often become attached to our reputations, possessions, and image. Indeed, these things drive our ambitions and aspirations, leading us to accumulate material comforts like homes, cars, and travel experiences. However, an excessive focus on materialism can be constraining; we may lose our sense of freedom and become preoccupied with achievements, image, and consumption. The essence of spirituality lies in transcending these time-bound preoccupations to connect with a profounder meaning and reality of our existence. This understanding cannot merely be acquired from books; it must be explored and experienced firsthand.

Contemplate the implications of this for leadership. If leaders are too engrossed in the material realm, it will dictate their leadership approach. While this can be effective to an extent, it can also render leaders reactive and defensive, particularly when facing threats to their materialistic values or when their self-images are challenged. An excessive attachment to oneself and one's image can hinder genuine teamwork, openness to change, and the ability to relish the present moment. Such leaders might find themselves perpetually busy, yet at a loss to determine the true value or meaning behind their endeavours. The voice that seeks deeper meaning or questions the worth of our pursuits is the call of our spiritual side. It beckons us to seek value and purpose beyond life's everyday ups and downs.

To further delve into these concepts, spend some time reflecting on the exercises below:

Cultivating Spiritual Wellbeing:

Examine the spiritual column in the table on the opposite page.

- What reactions do you have to the items listed?
- How can one develop their spiritual wellbeing?
- How might a person's wellbeing suffer if they haven't integrated spiritual wellbeing into their life?
- What barriers prevent you from exploring spiritual wellbeing? Where do these notions originate? What misconceptions might deter you from embracing spiritual wellbeing?

Now, consider the 'material' column in the table on the opposite page.

- How much of your life perspective is based on the items in this column?
- What are the strengths and pitfalls of being too aligned with material wellbeing?

Review both columns as complementary entities.

- How can material and spiritual wellbeing balance one another in an individual's life?
- Can you envisage situations where people lean too heavily on the material aspect, neglecting the spiritual, and vice versa?
- Contemplate strategies to ensure both material and spiritual well-being harmoniously coexist in your life.
- Ponder on the relationship between science and spirituality. Can these seemingly opposing realms coexist? What implications does this have for our predominantly scientific society?

Now that you know more about wellbeing polarities and believe that you, too, can make a positive difference in your life, the lives of others, and the world, what are you going to do with this knowledge?

Create a concept map below of the ideas and inspiring words that might drive your wellbeing in the future. We know you can do it!

Related **research**

Below is a list of publications reporting the direct research underpinning this book.

Mishra, A. (2022). How and Why Senior Managers Think Differently About Wellbeing: Towards a Constructive Developmental Theory. Unpublished PhD Dissertation, UQ Business School, University of Queensland.

Newey, L.R., de Oliveira, R.T., & Mishra, A. (2022). Wellbeing as a staged social responsibility process: Exploratory testing of a new theory. *Social Responsibility Journal*.

Newey, L.R. & Coenen, L. (2021). Lock-in, paradox and regional renewal. *Regional Studies,* 56(8), 1333-1346.

Newey, L. & de Oliveira, R.T. (2019). Wellbeing as emergent from the leveraging of polarities: Harnessing component interdependencies. *Social Indicators Research,* 144(2), 575-600.

Newey, L.R. (2019). Well-being as a staged social responsibility process for business and society. *Social Responsibility Journal,* 15(1), 75-89.

Newey, L.R. (2019). This mindset will help train a new generation of wellbeing leader. *Entrepreneur Asia Pacific,* May 18.

Newey, L.R. (2018). New paradigms for a complex world. *Strive Business Magazine.*

Acknowledgements

The research on which this book is based was funded by a forward-looking bunch of Brisbane schools committed to building wellbeing polarity leaders:

- Lois O'Reilly,
  Principal, Indooroopilly State High

- Llew Paulger,
  Executive Principal,
  Kelvin Grove State College

- Norm Kerley,
  Deputy Principal, John Paul College

- Damian Johnson,
  Principal, Ironside Primary

The authors are also indebted to Associate Professor Paul Spee and colleagues in the Strategy and Entrepreneurship Discipline at UQ Business School. Associate Professor Spee enabled funding of the development of the book, a sign of the commitment of the Strategy and Entrepreneurship Discipline to making its leading-edge research available for the benefit of others.

The authors would also like to acknowledge the hard work and dedication of our research partner Archana Mishra, whose PhD research also informed this book.

The authors are grateful to the Visible Thinking project at Project Zero, Harvard Graduate School of Education (pz.harvard.edu/thinking-routines).

Meet the **authors**

Dr Lance Newey is a Senior Lecturer in Social Entrepreneurship in the Strategy and Entrepreneurship Discipline at the University of Queensland Business School. He researches leading change through wellbeing approaches to business and society.

In putting the book together, Dr Lance says, 'To be able to teach effectively in a global institution requires confronting the limits of your own worldview. International students wanted better answers than I could give them, and the world was changing in ways that old teaching wasn't enough. In short, we weren't preparing leaders for a more complex world. I had to change and search for better answers. This book is the result of a quest to find better answers for the many amazing students who have walked into my classroom wanting to contribute to a better world.'

Dawn Boland (Cooper Hewitt Fellow, 2015) is a Lead Teacher in the areas of Design and Psychology. Her passion in her studies and research is to embed an Entrepreneurial Mindset within the curriculum through authentic and meaningful experiences for students. Dawn first encountered the Wellbeing Polarity Leadership Wheel through her enrolment in the Entrepreneurial Leadership Course as part of her Master's Degree at UQ.

'The perspectives presented about transformational leadership and how small shifts in our thinking can bring such positive change have brought a new energy into my life, into the conversations I have with colleagues and how I approach difficult situations. The knowledge is practical whilst bringing hope and confidence to approaches that don't aim to present band-aid solutions but enduring solutions that are adaptable and sustainable as the variables change.' She has enjoyed the experience of collaborating with Lance and Lara to bring Entrepreneurial Wellbeing Leadership alive for parents and students and says, 'This is the change I have been waiting for in our schools, to see practical and meaningful ways of solving the bigger problems and bringing wellbeing alive in our classrooms.'

Lara Berge is a penultimate year student at the University of Queensland. Her bachelor's degree in Advanced Business (Honours), majoring in Entrepreneurship and Innovation and Human Resources, reflects her passion for the intersections between psychology and business. Lara was introduced to the Wellbeing Polarity Leadership content as a student in Lance's undergraduate course.

As a current course facilitator, she 'hopes that all students can one day be exposed to the transformational content. The Wellbeing Polarity Leadership content has shifted how I view the world and people around me, including the way that I view myself. This has helped me to become a better leader, student, employee and person.'

Artwork by Bright Yellow

www.ingramcontent.com/pod-product-compliance
Lightning Source LLC
Chambersburg PA
CBHW042019090526
44590CB00029B/4341